DOCUMENTING HISTORY

THE CRUSADES
CHRISTIANS AT WAR

CHRISTINE HATT

FRANKLIN WATTS

A Division of Scholastic Inc.

NEW YORK TORONTO LONDON AUCKLAND SYDNEY

MEXICO CITY NEW DELHI HONG KONG

DANBURY, CONNECTICUT

First published by Evans Brothers Limited, 2000
2A Portman Mansions
Chiltern Street
London
W1M 1LE

© Evans Brothers Limited 2000

First American edition 2001 by Franklin Watts
A Division of Scholastic Inc.
90 Sherman Turnpike
Danbury, CT 06816

ISBN 0-531-14610-3 (Lib. Bdg)

Catalog details are available from the Library of Congress
Cataloging-in-Publication Data

Printed in Spain by GRAFO

Design – Neil Sayer
Editorial – Kath Davies
Maps – Tim Smith
Consultant – Professor Malcolm Barber
Production – Jenny Mulvanny

Title page picture: An illustration by Matthew Paris from a 13th-century manuscript, showing a battle at Damietta, Egypt, 1218

ACKNOWLEDGMENTS

For permission to reproduce copyright pictorial material, the author and publishers gratefully acknowledge the following:
cover (top left) Bridgeman Art Library (top right) the art archive (bottom right) Trip/C Rennie (bottom left) Bridgeman Art Library **title page** Corpus Christi College, Oxford/Bridgeman Art Library **page 7** British Library **page 8** e.t. archive **page 9** AKG London/Erich Lessing **page 10** Louvre, Paris/Bridgeman Art Library, London/New York **page 11** e.t. archive **page 12** (left) E Simanor/Robert Harding Picture Library (right) AKG/Erich Lessing **page 14** British Library **page 15** (left) e.t. archive (right) Ancient Art and Architecture Collection **page 16** AKG **page 17** Aleppo, Syria/Bridgeman Art Library **page 18** (top right) e. t. archive (bottom left) e.t. archive **page 19** British Library/Bridgeman Art Library **page 21** British Library/Bridgeman Art Library **page 22** British Library/Bridgeman Art Library **page 24** (top) AKG (bottom) e.t. archive **page 25** Robert Harding Picture Library **page 26** British Library **page 27** Ancient Art and Architecture **page 28** Trip/C Rennie **page 29** Bibliotheque Nationale, Paris/Bridgeman Art Library **page 30** Robert Harding Picture Library **page 32** (top right) British Library/Bridgeman Art Library (bottom) Chateau de Versailles, France/Lauros-Giraudon/Bridgeman Art Library **page 33** With thanks to The Order of St Johns, London **page 34** (top right) Mary Evans Picture Library (bottom left) Bibliotheque Nationale, Paris/Bridgeman Art Library **page 35** Robert Harding Picture Library **page 36** Bibliotheque Nationale, Paris **page 38** (top left) Bibliotheque Municipale de Lyon/Bridgeman Art Library (bottom right) AKG **page 40** Chris Barton **page 41** Robert Harding Picture Library/Odyssey/Chicago **page 42** Mary Evans Picture Library **page 43** Fred Friberg/Robert harding Picture Library **page 44** (top right) e.t. archive (bottom left) British Library/Bridgeman Art Library **page 45** British Library **page 46** AKG **page 47** The Governing Body of Christ Church, Oxford **page 48** (top right) AKG (bottom) e.t.archive **page 49** Michael Venner/Robert Harding Picture Library **page 50** (top) AKG (bottom) Robert Harding Picture Library **page 51** Palazzo Ducale, Venice/Bridgeman Art Library **page 52** British Library **page 53** British Library/Bridgeman Art Library **page 54** (top) Corpus Christi College, Oxford/Bridgeman Art Library (bottom) e.t. archive **page 55** Biblioteca Apostolica Vaticana, The Vatican/Bridgeman Art Library **page 56** (top right) e.t.archive (bottom left) AKG **page 57** Mary Evans Picture Library **page 58** e.t.archive **page 59** With thanks to The Order of St John, London

For permission to reproduce copyright material for the documents, the author and publisher gratefully acknowledge the following:
page 13 The Innocent's Abroad, Mark Twain, Oxford University Press 1996 **page 17, 21, 35, 37** (bottom), **39, 43** (top), **49** (bottom), **51, 53** Chronicles of the Crusades, Eye-witness accounts of the wars between Christianity and Islam, Quadrillion Publishing, 1996 **page 19** and **page 31** (bottom) A History of the Expedition to Jerusalem 1095-1127 translated by Frances Rita Ryan and edited by Harold S Fink, University of Tennessee Press, 1969 **page 23, 27** (bottom), **35, 37** (top), **41** (top), **45** (top and bottom), **47** (top), **49** (top), **55** Arab Historians of the Crusades - Selected and translated from the Arabic Sources. Edited/translated by E. J. Costello. Copyright © 1969 Routledge & Kegan Paul Ltd. **page 25** and **27** (top) The Deeds of the Franks and other Pilgrims to Jerusalem (Gesta Francorum et aliorum Hierosolimitanorum) edited by Rosalind Hill, Thomas Nelson and Sons Ltd **page 31** (top), An Arab-Syrian Gentleman and Warrior in the Period of the Crusades, (Memoirs of Usamah ibn Munqidh), translated by Philip K. Hitti Columbia Press 1929 **page 39** (top) De profectione Ludovici VII in Orientem (The Journey of Louis VII to the East), Odo of Deuil, Edited with an English Translation by Virginia Gingerick Berry, Columbia Press 1948 **page 33** The Order of St John, London **page 43** (bottom) Reproduced from Crusades by Alan Ereira and Terry Jones with permission of BBC Worldwide Limited © Fegg Features Ltd and Alan Ereira 1994

CONTENTS

LOOKING AT DOCUMENTS

In A.D. 1095, Pope Urban II appealed for fighters to go to the Holy Land to free it from Muslim control. The response was overwhelming. No one then realized that Urban had launched a bitter and bloody struggle between Christians and Muslims that would last for centuries.

The wars of these years are known as crusades, from the Latin *crux*, meaning "cross," the symbol of Christianity. This book examines the eight crusades that began in hope in 1095 and ended in disillusion in 1270. It also looks at the states set up by crusaders in the Middle East and the reasons for their destruction.

During this era, Popes also launched crusades against heretical Christians such as the Cathars of southern France, against Muslims in Spain, and against pagans in northern Europe. You can find out about these conflicts in this book, too.

To bring these stories to life, *The Crusades* uses a wide range of documents, from the works of Christian and Muslim chroniclers to the rules of religious orders. To make the documents easier to read, they are printed in modern type. You will also find photographs of some of the original documents. Difficult or old-fashioned words and phrases are explained in labels.

When you look at these documents, think about their origins. When were they written—in the early days of the crusades, when those taking part were full of enthusiasm, or toward the end, when they were weary? Where were they written—from a distance or in the Holy Land itself? Above all, who wrote them? Christian and Muslim views of an event were often very different. The answers to these and similar questions will help you decide how reliable each document is likely to be. But no single document can give a complete picture, and people involved in a situation may not understand it as well as those looking back many years later.

On these pages are excerpts from documents used in this book. They show the variety of documents included, and explain how and why the documents were written.

Some writers recorded their first-hand experiences of the crusades in diaries. After the Second Crusade, French monk Odo of Deuil turned his notes about the expedition into a book (see page 39). This excerpt describes how Abbot Bernard of Clairvaux first preached the crusade to the waiting crowds.

Bernard, speaking as inspired by God.

... since there was no place within the town which could accommodate such a large crowd, a wooden platform was erected outside in a field ... [Bernard] mounted the platform accompanied by the king, who was wearing the cross; and when **heaven's instrument** poured forth the dew of the divine word ... with loud outcry people on every side began to demand crosses. And when he had **sowed** ... the parcel of crosses which had been prepared beforehand, he was forced to tear his own garments into crosses and to sow them abroad...

Bernard had to throw them into the crowd like seed rather than hand them out.

Many other people who wrote histories of the crusades were not personally involved in the events they described. Instead, they collected information from a variety of sources, such as eyewitnesses and books, to produce their own accounts. The Syrian Muslim Kamal ad-Din, for example, wrote this powerful description of the "Field of Blood" battle about 100 years after it took place in 1119 (see page 35).

… God gave victory to the Muslims. The Franks who fled to their camp were slaughtered. The Turks fought superbly… Arrows flew thick as locusts, and the Franks, with missiles raining down on infantry and cavalry alike, … fled.

Several of the documents in this book are concerned not with great events and personalities but with daily life. Here, Muslim writer Usama ibn Munqidh explains how some crusaders who settled in the Middle East adopted Islamic beliefs and customs (see page 31).

and we came to the house of one of the old knights who came with the first expedition … He had a fine table brought out, spread with a splendid selection of appetizing food. He saw that I was not eating, and said: "Don't worry, please; eat what you like, for I don't eat Frankish food. I have Egyptian cooks and eat only what they serve. No pig's flesh ever comes into my house!" …

Islam forbids the eating of pork.

THE MUSLIM CALENDAR

The dates in this book are given according to the Christian calendar, whose years are counted from the (approximate) birth of Christ. However, it is important to know that Muslims use a different dating system. The Muslim calendar began in the year 622 of the Christian era, on the day Muhammad fled from his enemies in Mecca (see page 11). It is based on the cycles of the moon, and each of its years contains 354 days instead of the 365 days of the Christian system.

A battle plan showing troop positions from one of Saladin's manuals (see page 45).

ORIGINS
THE CHRISTIAN WORLD

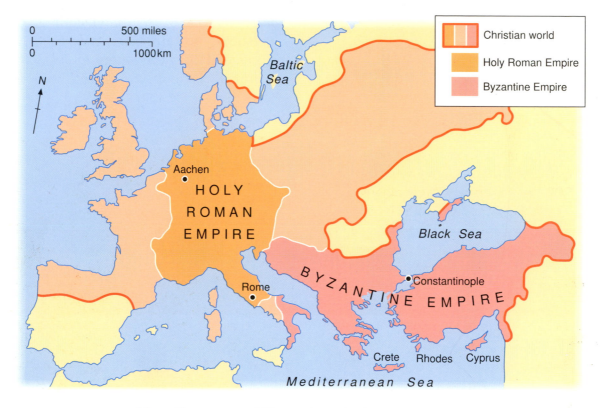

THE CHRISTIAN WORLD IN ABOUT A.D. 1050

In A.D. 330, Constantine, the first Christian Roman emperor, left Rome and set up a second imperial capital in the Greek colony of Byzantium, to the east. The city was renamed Constantinople after its new ruler. It became the center of a magnificent civilization, combining Greek and Roman cultures. At its heart was the Christian faith, based on the teachings of Jesus Christ (see box).

While Constantinople went from strength to strength, the Roman Empire in the West declined as Asian and Germanic tribes poured across its borders. In 410 the invaders sacked Rome, and in 476 the last Roman emperor was removed. Despite these political changes, the Roman Catholic Church, centered in Rome, maintained its position.

This illustration from an 11th-century edition of the Christian Gospels shows the Roman emperor Constantine (left) and his mother, Helena.

The head of the church, the Pope, claimed authority over all Christians. However, many Christians in the east regarded the Patriarch of Constantinople as their religious leader.

In 1054, the split between the western (Roman Catholic) and eastern (Greek Orthodox) branches of the church was made official. By that time, Constantinople controlled a huge area known as the Byzantine Empire. Despite losses to the Arabs in the 7th century (see pages 10-11), the empire stretched from southern Italy in the west to Mesopotamia in the east. Constantinople itself was home to about half a million people and contained many beautiful buildings, including the Church of Hagia Sophia (Holy Wisdom), which was built from 532 to 537 for the Byzantine emperor Justinian.

Western Europe recovered slowly from centuries of decay following the collapse of the Roman Empire. In 800, a ruler named Charlemagne established a new political unit, later known as the Western or Holy Roman Empire, with its capital at Aachen in what is now Germany. He reunited much of Europe, encouraged a revival of learning, and promoted Roman Catholic Christianity. Yet 11th-century Western Europe could not compare with the splendor of Byzantium. However, important changes were under way (see pages 14-15).

CHRIST AND CHRISTIANITY

Jesus Christ was a Jew who lived in Palestine from about 4 B.C. to A.D. 30. The New Testament of the Bible records that Jesus (shown in a Byzantine mosaic below) emphasized God's love for humanity and the need for people to love God and one another.

By the 11th century, there were many Christian groups, each with its own interpretation of Christian teaching. In their journeys, the Catholic crusaders met not only Greek Orthodox Christians, but also Jacobites, Armenians, Maronites, and others. Despite Christ's example of non-violence, these groups often fought among themselves.

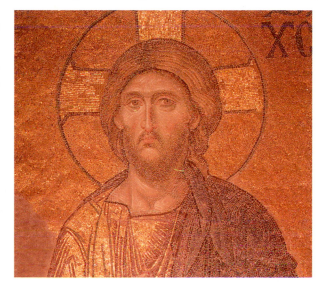

 Chapters 5-7 of St. Matthew's Gospel in the New Testament tell how Jesus preached one day on a hillside. The themes of the Sermon on the Mount are love, humility, and self-sacrifice. This is an excerpt from the sermon:

... You have heard that it was said, "Love your neighbor and hate your enemy. But I tell you: Love your enemies and pray for those who persecute you, that you may be sons of your Father in heaven. He causes his sun to rise on the evil and the good, and sends rain on the righteous and the unrighteous. If you love those who love you, what reward will you get? Are not even the tax collectors doing that? And if you greet only your brothers, what are you doing more than others? Do not even pagans do that? Be perfect, therefore, as your heavenly Father is perfect." (Matthew 5, verses 43-48)

Jesus taught his followers to see God as their Father.

THE ISLAMIC WORLD

The religion of Islam was first preached by the Prophet Muhammad, who lived in Arabia from A.D. 570 to 632 (see box). Its followers are called Muslims. Islam spread across much of the Arabian Peninsula, then north and west, taking over Byzantine territories in Palestine, Syria, and North Africa, and east into Persia and India. In A.D. 711, Muslims invaded Spain and soon controlled all but the north of that country.

Following Muhammad's death, the Islamic world was governed by a caliph, who had both religious and political powers. The first caliph was Abu Bakr, Muhammad's father-in-law. One group of Muslims, the Sunnis, acknowledged his right to the role, but a second group, the Shi'ites, believed that Ali, the Prophet's son-in-law, should rule. Sunni and Shi'ite Muslims remained divided, developing different views on Islamic doctrine and practice.

The caliphate passed to the Sunni Umayyad family, who ruled from Damascus. In 750, they were overthrown by the mighty Abbasid dynasty, which governed from Baghdad. In 909, a rival Shi'ite dynasty, the Fatimids, emerged in North Africa. They conquered Egypt, founded Cairo about 1000, and governed a second Islamic empire from that city.

This illustrated page from a 16th-century Qur'an shows the Archangel Gabriel appearing to the Prophet Muhammad.

THE ISLAMIC WORLD ABOUT A.D. 1050

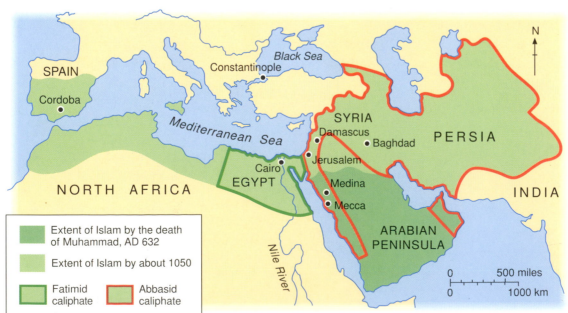

- Extent of Islam by the death of Muhammad, AD 632
- Extent of Islam by about 1050
- Fatimid caliphate
- Abbasid caliphate

SPAIN
Cordoba
Black Sea
Constantinople
Mediterranean Sea
NORTH AFRICA
Cairo
EGYPT
Nile River
SYRIA
Damascus
Jerusalem
Baghdad
Medina
Mecca
PERSIA
INDIA
ARABIAN PENINSULA

0   500 miles
0   1000 km

The cities of the Islamic world, with their mosques, bazaars, and palaces, rivaled Constantinople. Baghdad, for example, was a center of religion, trade, and culture. Its university, the House of Wisdom, was founded in 830. There, Arab scholars translated and discussed the works of ancient Greek scientists and philosophers. They made brilliant discoveries in mathematics, medicine, and astronomy.

Jews and Christians lived alongside Muslims in these great cities. Islam classed them as "people of the book," whose holy writings had come from God and whose religions therefore contained some truth. For this reason, they were treated with tolerance, but they had to pay a special tax, the *jizya*, from which Muslims were exempt.

The brilliant Arab doctor and scholar Ibn Sina (known in the West as Avicenna) lived from 980 to 1037. Students flocked to hear his teaching.

MUHAMMAD AND ISLAM

The Prophet Muhammad was born in Mecca in present-day Saudi Arabia. In A. D. 610, he had the first of many visions in which the Archangel Gabriel gave him messages from God. Muhammad began to preach a new religion, Islam, based on these revelations. Islam taught people to worship one God, Allah, to pray regularly, and to act justly. It also taught that Muhammad was the last of many prophets sent by God, among whom was Jesus, known to Muslims as *Isa*.

Many people in Mecca opposed Muhammad's teachings, and he fled north to Medina in 622. This event is known as the *Hejira* (flight). In 630, Muhammad's armies finally defeated the Meccans. The Prophet died in Medina in 632.

Muhammad's revelations are written in the Muslim holy book, the Qur'an ("Reading"). It teaches that *jihad* (fighting) may be necessary.

Like Christianity, Islam teaches that when the world ends, everyone will be judged by God.

"Apostle" here means Muhammad.

... Fighting is obligatory for you, much as you dislike it. But you may hate a thing although it is good for you, and love a thing although it is bad for you. God knows, but you know not ... (Qur'an 2:216)

... Fight against such of those to whom the Scriptures were given as belief in neither God nor the **Last Day**, who do not forbid what God and his **Apostle** have forbidden, and do not embrace the true Faith, until they pay tribute out of hand and are utterly subdued ... (Qur'an 9:29)

JERUSALEM

The city of Jerusalem, in present-day Israel, is sacred to three religions. To Jewish people it is the capital of the first united Jewish kingdom, set up by King David in 1000 B.C. It was also the site of the temple built by David's son, Solomon, about fifty years later. By the time of the crusades, this temple had long been destroyed. But a wall from a later temple, destroyed in A.D. 70, remains a place of pilgrimage.

For Christians, Jerusalem is holy because Jesus Christ spent the last days of his earthly life there, and his crucifixion took place just outside its walls. The Mount of Olives, to the east of the city, is believed to be the site of his ascension into heaven. Pilgrims visit Jerusalem's holy places, including Jesus's tomb, over which Byzantine Christians built the Church of the Holy Sepulchre in the 4th century.

Today Muslims pray facing Mecca, where the Prophet Muhammad was born (see pages 10-11). However, until 624 they faced Jerusalem, which they regarded as a holy city. According to Muslim belief, the Prophet Muhammad was led to Jerusalem by the Archangel Gabriel during his Night Journey. There he saw the earlier prophets, then ascended into heaven, where he was granted a vision of God. This event made Jerusalem even more sacred to Muslims.

In the early 7th century, Jerusalem was under Byzantine control, and disaster threatened the Christians. In 634, Omar, a former adviser to Muhammad, became the second caliph of the Islamic empire. In 638, after besieging the city for more than a year, Omar claimed Jerusalem, bringing in four hundred years of Muslim rule.

The magnificent mosque known as the Dome of the Rock was built on the site of Solomon's Temple in Jerusalem during the late 7th century.

Jerusalem's Church of the Holy Sepulchre today. Inside, the main area of the church is circular, and many Western churches built during the crusading era followed this design.

Under Omar and his Abbasid successors, the non-Muslims of Jerusalem were allowed to practice their own religions in peace. However, in 969, the Fatimids took over the city, and the atmosphere grew more hostile. Under Caliph al-Hakim's rule (996–1021), serious persecution of both Christians and Jews began. In 1004, he ordered the destruction of many churches, and in 1009, the Church of the Holy Sepulchre itself was burned down. The rights and property of Christians were later restored, and the Byzantines were allowed to rebuild the Church of the Holy Sepulchre. Once again, pilgrims poured into the city. But a new threat was not far away (see pages 16-17).

Palestine Pilgrims' Text Society.

DIARY OF A JOURNEY THROUGH SYRIA AND PALESTINE.

BY
NÂSIR-I-KHUSRAU,
IN 1047 A.D.

TRANSLATED FROM THE PERSIAN AND ANNOTATED BY
GUY LE STRANGE.

LONDON:
24, HANOVER SQUARE, W.
1896.

The Persian traveler-poet Nasir-i Khusrau set out in 1046 on a pilgrimage to Mecca. In his *Diary of a Journey through Syria and Palestine,* published in English in 1896, he describes Jerusalem.

... Anyone of that province [Syria] who cannot perform the pilgrimage to **Mecca** will visit Jerusalem ... Christians and Jews in large numbers [come] to worship at the church and **synagogue** there ... the Holy City [is] set on a hill ... Strong walls of stone and mortar with gates of iron surround the city. It is a **populous** place which, when I saw it, contained twenty thousand people. There are fine bazaars and many tall buildings, and all the streets are paved in stone.

The pilgrimage to Mecca, the *hajj,* is one of every Muslim's five main duties. Muslims try to go there at least once in their lifetime.

"Containing a large number of people."

A building where Jews worship and teach their religion.

Christians make pilgrimages to Jerusalem's Church of the Holy Sepulchre. American author Samuel Langhorne Clemens, better known as Mark Twain, described his visit there in *The Innocents Abroad* (1869):

The areas of the world in which Christianity is the main religion.

... we stand before the most sacred locality in **Christendom**—the grave of Jesus. ... Stooping low, we enter the vault—the Sepulchre itself. It is only about six feet by seven, and the stone couch on which the dead Savior lay extends from end to end of the apartment and occupies half its width. It is covered with a marble slab which has been much worn by the lips of pilgrims...

MEDIEVAL EUROPE

Medieval Europe suffered a steady stream of invasions, from Goths in the 4th and 5th centuries, to Vikings from the 8th. The society that developed in the early Middle Ages was therefore based largely on the need for defense.

Most European states of this period were headed by a monarch or emperor. These rulers were not all-powerful and could not afford large, well-equipped armies. So they granted estates to local lords in return for their loyalty and the provision of soldiers in time of war. The lords in turn granted land to the fighters who served

them. From about A.D. 900, many of these men were knights. At first, knights were simply soldiers who fought on horseback. By the 11th century, they formed an upper class, because only rich nobles and princes had the money to buy horses and armor.

Working people, the peasants, held small plots of land that belonged to lords, knights, or the church. It was their task to grow food for all, working their own plots and their lord's lands. Their years were an unceasing round of tending crops and animals, and their homes were usually small,

one-roomed huts. Disease and hunger were part of their lives, often ending them abruptly and painfully. In the 11th century, their situation was improving slightly. New farming methods and better harvests brought larger, healthier populations.

From the 10th century, the Roman Catholic Church increased in religious and political power. Its attitude toward violence, which Jesus had opposed, also changed. Many church leaders began to preach that fighting was acceptable in a just cause, such as the protection of the weak or the punishment of the wicked. Finally, during the papacy of Gregory VII (1073–85), the church decided that it was right to fight in defense of Christianity. As a result, knights gained a new image as courageous "soldiers of Christ."

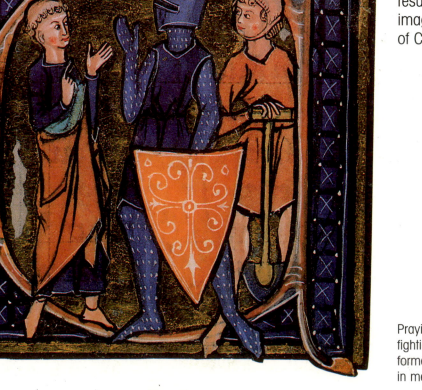

Praying monks, nuns, and priests; fighting knights; and working peasants formed the three main groups of society in medieval Europe.

The 12th-century philosopher John of Salisbury, who became Bishop of Chartres in France, described the role of the knight.

... What is the function of orderly knighthood? To protect the church, to fight against treachery, to reverence the priesthood, to fend off injustice from the poor, to make peace in your own province, to shed blood for your brethren, and if needs must, to lay down your life ...

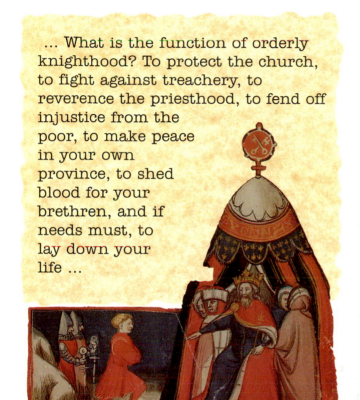

A king performs the accolade, the ceremonial touch on the shoulder by which a man was made a knight.

RELIGIOUS REVIVAL

Three new monastic orders, all founded in France, encouraged spiritual revival within the Roman Catholic Church during the early Middle Ages. The Cluniacs set up their first monastery at Cluny (below) in 910, the strict Carthusians at Chartreuse in 1084, and the Cistercians at Cîteaux in 1098. Many people made pilgrimages to the Holy Land.

Noble families had their sons trained for knighthood from the age of seven. Knighting involved a touch on the shoulder with fist or sword, when the words "Be thou a knight" were spoken. It might be part of a religious ceremony when the knight's sword was blessed.

This German blessing dates from the mid-10th century, and was also used in England and France. It shows the church's approval of violence in "just" causes.

Hearken, we beseech Thee, O Lord, to our prayers, and **deign to** bless with the right hand of Thy majesty this sword with which this Thy servant desires to be girded, that it may be a defense of churches, widows, orphans, and all Thy servants against the scourge of the pagans, that it may be the terror and dread of other evildoers, and that it may be just both in attack and defense ..

"Deign to" means "be good enough to."

THE SELJUK TURKS

In the mid-11th century, a new and aggressive Sunni Muslim power, the Seljuk Turks, began a series of conquests. In 1055, they took Baghdad from the Abbasids, and in 1071 drove the Fatimids from Jerusalem. Their goal was the magnificent city of Constantinople.

On August 19, 1071, Seljuks and Byzantines clashed in a great battle at Manzikert in present-day Turkey. At the head of the Seljuk army was Sultan Alp-Arslan, while Emperor Romanus IV Diogenes led the Byzantine troops. The Byzantine army was badly equipped but vast, containing about 100,000 fighters. Most of these soldiers were mercenaries, who felt no great commitment to the Byzantine cause. When the Seljuk sultan launched his attack, the Byzantines were catastrophically defeated.

THE BYZANTINE AND SELJUK EMPIRES IN A. D. 1095

Following their victory at the Battle of Manzikert, the Turks advanced deep into Byzantine territory. Sultan Alp-Arslan was succeeded by his son, the mighty Malik Shah, in 1072.

Twenty years later, the Seljuk empire stretched from northern India in the east to within a few miles of Constantinople in the west. In Constantinople itself, defeat at Manzikert was followed by brutal civil war.

After the death of Malik Shah in 1092, a struggle for power led to the division of the Seljuk empire into sultanates and emirates. Some, such as the Sultanate of Rum, covered huge areas. Others, including the Emirates of Damascus and Aleppo, were large and powerful cities with surrounding land. Each had its own ruler who ruthlessly pursued his own objectives.

An early (1400s) map of Constantinople.

The massive citadel that still stands outside the town of Aleppo in Syria was built in the early 13th century.

Emperor Romanus fought bravely at Manzikert, but was wounded and captured. This account is taken from *Histories* by the Byzantine writer Nicephorus Bryennius, the husband of Anna Comnena (see pages 20-21). Bryennius's grandfather fought in the battle.

... Recognized by the enemy, hemmed in on all sides, he was captured when an arrow wounded his horse, which slipped and lost its footing, felling its rider at the same time.

So it was that Emperor Romanus became a prisoner of war and was led bound to Sultan Alp-Arslan ... As to the rest, some were slaughtered, others managed to save themselves. The whole camp was taken, along with the imperial tent, the treasure and the most beautiful among the crown jewels, including the famous pearl called the Orpheline...

THE ASSASSINS

Malik Shah was a follower of the Sunni branch of Islam. In 1090, a Shi'ite sect was set up to oppose him and Sunnism as a whole. Its founder was a Persian, Hasan as-Sabah, who resented the Seljuk conquest of his country. In his stronghold high in the Syrian mountains, he taught not only his version of Islam but also the techniques of political murder.

Hasan's terrorists became known as *hashishi*, because they were believed to take the drug hashish before their murderous missions. In the West, they were known by another form of this word—assassins.

THE FIRST CRUSADE
THE CALL TO CRUSADE

In 1081, a new ruler came to power in Byzantium—Emperor Alexius Comnenus. During his reign, the Byzantine Empire steadily shrank as Malik Shah forced his way west. By the 1090s, Byzantine fortunes were improving while the divided Turks were in decline. Nevertheless, Constantinople was still in danger.

Alexius aimed to end the Seljuk threat, but first he needed a substantial army. However, Anatolia (present-day Turkey), where Byzantine rulers had previously recruited many soldiers, was now under Seljuk control. So in 1095, Alexius sent ambassadors to Pope Urban II for help. The emperor hoped for the assistance of highly trained mercenaries to drive back the Turks. But the Pope had a grander enterprise in mind.

In November 1095, Urban presided over a ten-day meeting of clergy in Clermont, France.

Pope Urban II

A public meeting was called for November 27, at which an important announcement would be made. So many people came that the chosen venue, Clermont Cathedral, had to be abandoned. Instead, Urban's fateful speech was made in a field outside the city walls.

In his speech, the Pope told of Alexius's appeal and explained the need to repel the Turks. Above all, he emphasized Christians' sacred duty to free the Holy Land, and particularly Jerusalem, from Seljuk control. Urban portrayed the Turks as bloodthirsty infidels, who killed local Christians and visiting pilgrims alike. He also promised that anyone who died fighting to

Pope Urban II preaching to clergy at Clermont Cathedral in 1095.

free the Holy Land would have their sins forgiven and win a place in heaven.

Urban spoke freely of the religious reasons why people should take up arms against the Turks. He did not mention another of his own objectives. By organizing an expedition to the Holy Land, then taking over this sacred territory, he hoped to bring all Christians, Orthodox as well as Catholic, under his control.

Even before Urban had finished speaking, it became clear that he had unleashed powerful emotions among his listeners. The crowds cheered their support, and many immediately promised to head for the East. The crusading movement was under way.

 Five accounts of Pope Urban's speech in Clermont have survived. None is an exact record, but they all agree on his themes. This excerpt comes from the Latin *Historia Hierosolymitana* by Fulcher of Chartres. Fulcher was chaplain to Baldwin, one of the leaders of the First Crusade (see pages 22-23). In 1916 an English translation, *A History of the Expedition to Jerusalem 1095-1127*, was published. This extract comes from it:

TAKING THE CROSS

Crusaders made a public vow in front of a priest stating that they were going to war "in God's cause." They were presented with a cross, as a symbol of the Christian faith. These crosses were often made of red fabric. Knights attached them to the tunics, known as surcoats, that they wore over their armor (see picture below). Some people, however, branded crosses directly onto their skin.

"Begged."

2. ... you must hasten to carry aid to your brethren dwelling in the East, who need your help, for which they have often **entreated**.

3. For the Turks ... have seized more and more of the lands of the Christians, ... have killed or captured many people, have destroyed churches, and have devastated the kingdom of God. If you allow them to continue much longer they will conquer God's faithful people much more extensively.

4. Wherefore with earnest prayer I, not I, but God **exhorts** you as heralds of Christ to ... urge men of all ranks whatsoever, knights as well as foot-soldiers, rich and poor, to hasten to exterminate this vile race from our lands and to aid the Christian inhabitants in time.

"Urgently requests."

THE PEOPLE'S CRUSADE

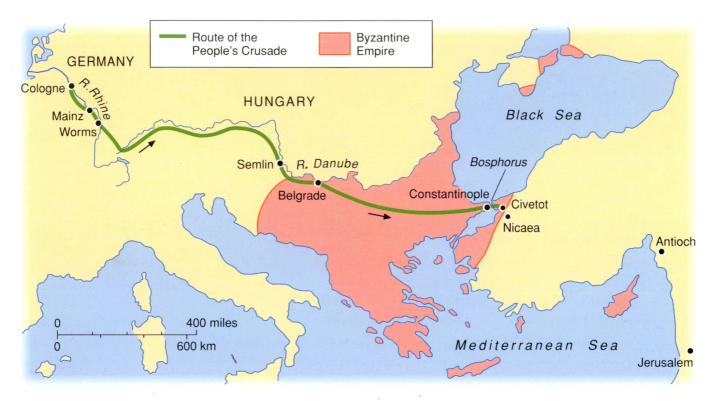

THE PEOPLE'S CRUSADE

From late 1095, penniless monks began to tour France and Germany. Their powerful preaching in support of the crusade produced a religious frenzy among thousands of peasants. By late 1095, the peasants' situation was especially bad, following recent drought and famine. Population increases (see pages 14-15) had resulted in a shortage of land to grow food. If they stayed where they were, peasants faced poverty and hunger. If they fought for the Holy Land, they were guaranteed entrance to heaven. What was there to lose?

The most influential of the wandering monks was a Frenchman known as Peter the Hermit, whose preaching set people's hearts on fire. Peter tapped into the common belief that Jesus would soon return, punishing the evil and rewarding the good. Hordes of people—men, including some knights, women, even children—joined Peter on his travels. In April 1096, a crowd of about 20,000 people left Cologne in Germany for Constantinople, on their way to the Holy Land.

Peter had no idea how to control his so-called People's Crusade. They created havoc on their journey through Central Europe, killing four thousand people in the Hungarian town of Semlin, then sacking the Byzantine city of Belgrade. Jewish communities also suffered terribly at their hands (see box). Eventually, Emperor Alexius had to send troops to escort these crusaders to Constantinople.

The crusaders reached the city on August 1, 1096. Five days later they were transported across the Bosphorus into Asia, and surged into Turkish territory. In September, one group of crusaders captured the Turkish castle of Xerigordon. The Turks then cut off the water supply, forcing them to surrender or die. When they surrendered, only those who converted to Islam escaped with their lives. In October, the remaining crusaders were ambushed near their camp at Civetot. Few of them survived. The People's Crusade had been crushed.

THE FATE OF THE JEWS

Many crusaders had borrowed money from Jews to finance their expeditions to the East. They felt bitter at being in debt to people whom they regarded as Christ's enemies. This bitterness probably triggered their merciless attacks on Jews in northern France and German cities such as Mainz and Worms. They forgot that Jesus and many of his followers were Jews themselves.

In this 14th-century illustration, Peter the Hermit encourages women and men of the People's Crusade.

Peter the Hermit.

Turks.

Anna Comnena, daughter of Alexius, tried to kill her brother John so that her husband could inherit her father's throne. She was sent away to a convent, where she wrote *The Alexiad*. Written in Greek, it is a flattering, fascinating account of her father's reign. This is how Anna told the story of Peter the Hermit.

Western Christians.

... A divine voice, **he** said, commanded him to proclaim ... that all should ... with all their soul and might strive to liberate Jerusalem from the **Agarenes**. ... It was as if he had inspired every heart with some divine oracle. **Kelts** assembled from all parts ... with arms and horses and all the other equipment for war. Full of enthusiasm and ardor they thronged every highway, and with these warriors came a host of civilians, outnumbering the sand of the sea shore or the stars of heaven, carrying palms and bearing crosses on their shoulders. There were women and children, too, who had left their own countries ...

This is how a historian of the First Crusade, Abbot Guibert of Nogent, described Peter the Hermit:

... whatever he did or said seemed almost godlike, to such a degree that hairs were pulled from his mule as relics ... He used to wear the simplest woolen tunic, with a hooded cape over it, both down to his ankles, and over that, without sleeves, a cloak, and he went barefoot. He lived on wine and fish, bread rarely or never ...

THE OFFICIAL CRUSADE

By August 1096, five main armies were massing in Europe. Hugh of Vermandois, brother of King Philip I of France, commanded the first army to set out for the Holy Land. Godfrey of Bouillon and his brothers Baldwin and Eustace followed. Bohemond and his nephew Tancred then led out a force of Normans from Italy, followed by the largest army, under Raymond of Toulouse. Bringing up the rear were Normans from France, led by Robert of Normandy, Robert of Flanders and Stephen of Blois.

When the crusading armies arrived in Constantinople, Emperor Alexius made them swear an oath of allegiance to ensure that they fought for the good of Byzantium and not for their own gain. They promised to return any former Byzantine lands they won from the Turks, and to accept his rule over any new conquests. Many lords tried to avoid making

The siege of Antioch. The man second from the left is probably Bishop Adhémar of Le Puy, the Pope's representative on the First Crusade.

THE OFFICIAL CRUSADE

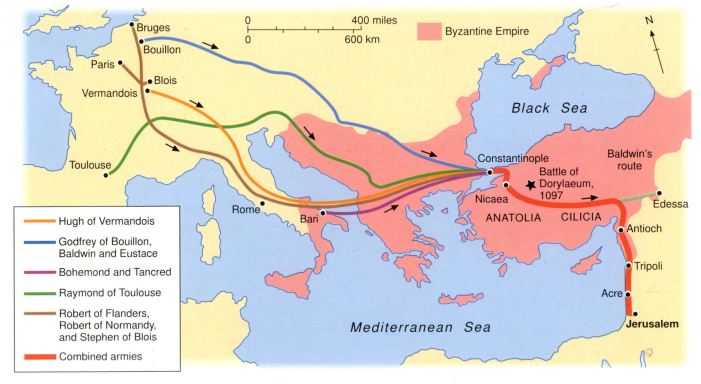

- Hugh of Vermandois
- Godfrey of Bouillon, Baldwin and Eustace
- Bohemond and Tancred
- Raymond of Toulouse
- Robert of Flanders, Robert of Normandy, and Stephen of Blois
- Combined armies

Byzantine Empire

0   400 miles
0   600 km

Bruges
Bouillon
Paris
Blois
Vermandois
Toulouse
Rome
Bari

Black Sea
Constantinople
Nicaea
Battle of Dorylaeum, 1097
Baldwin's route
Edessa
ANATOLIA   CILICIA
Antioch
Tripoli
Acre
Jerusalem

Mediterranean Sea

N

this commitment, as they hoped to carve out states for themselves in the Middle East. Eventually, they gave in.

After crossing into Asia, the crusaders defeated Seljuk troops at the Battle of Dorylaeum on July 1, 1097. After an arduous march across Anatolia, they were welcomed by the Armenian Christians of Cilicia. Baldwin then set out for Edessa, the richest Armenian town. He offered its ruler, Thoros, help against the Turks on condition that Thoros made him his heir. Thoros agreed, and was killed during a revolt a month later. So in March 1098, Baldwin became Count of Edessa, and Edessa became the first Crusader State (see pages 28-29).

Meanwhile, since October 1097, other crusaders had been laying siege to Antioch. In June 1098, an Armenian let Bohemond and his troops into the city. Every Muslim and many Christian inhabitants were slaughtered. Then a Muslim army led by Kerbogha, Emir of Mosul, appeared and besieged the crusaders in turn. The crusaders, starving and weak, seemed doomed. But apparent miracles and visions re-inspired them to defeat Kerbogha.

COUNTING THE COST

Knights had to make arrangements for the care of their land before going on crusade. They also had to buy horses, armor, and weapons and food and provide wages for the servants who accompanied them. Some knights even sold their estates to raise funds.

There were human costs, too. Many men were greatly distressed to leave their wives and children, whom they might never see again. Before he departed, Stephen of Blois donated a wood to a French abbey, "... so that God ... might ... lead me on the journey out of my homeland and bring me back healthy and safe, and watch over my wife Adela and our children."

According to their oath, the crusaders should have returned Antioch to Alexius. However, Bohemond claimed the city since he had organized its capture, and Antioch became the second Crusader State.

Ibn Al-Athir wrote a complete history of the Muslim world called *Kamil at-Tawarikh* (The Perfect History). Born in 1160, he had no direct experience of the First Crusade. He gave detailed, though not entirely accurate, accounts of the crusades from a Muslim point of view. Here he explains how Antioch was betrayed to the crusaders.

The Muslims called all Western European Christians Franks.

Armor that protects the chest and back.

... After the siege had been going on for a long time the **Franks** made a deal with ... a **cuirass-maker** called Ruzbih whom they bribed with a fortune in money and lands. He worked in the tower that stood over the **river-bed**, where the river flowed out of the city into the valley. The Franks ... made their way to the water-gate. They opened it and entered the city. Another gang of them climbed the tower with ropes. At dawn, when more than 500 of them were in the city and the defenders were worn out after the night watch, they sounded their trumpets...**They** sacked [the city] slaughtering all the Muslims they found there. ...

Antioch stands on the River Orontes.

The other crusaders.

THE CAPTURE OF JERUSALEM

After taking Antioch, some crusaders, including Hugh of Vermandois and his army, returned home. The rest turned south toward the greatest prize, Jerusalem. This involved a long journey through Turkish-held territory into Palestine, now ruled by the Egyptian Fatimids.

The first major battle on the way occurred in late 1098, at Maarat an-Numan in Syria. A two-week siege led to a terrible massacre of its inhabitants, after which the crusaders burned the city. The march south continued under the leadership of Raymond of Toulouse. With Raymond went

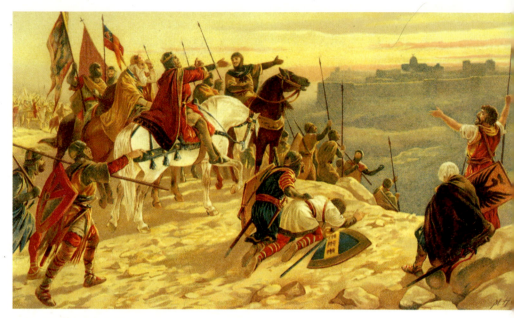

A romantic, early 20th-century illustration showing the knights of the First Crusade on the approach to Jerusalem.

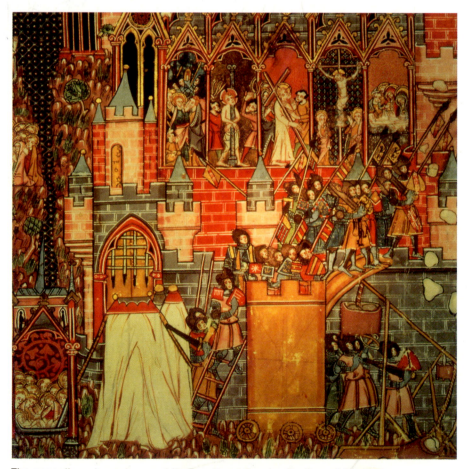

The assault on Jerusalem and its Egyptian rulers by Godfrey of Bouillon's troops in July 1099.

Tancred and Robert of Normandy. Robert of Flanders and Godfrey of Bouillon followed about a month later.

Many detours meant that the remaining 310-mi (500-km) journey to Jerusalem took six months. Finally, on June 7, 1099, the crusading armies, about 20,000 strong, set up camp outside Jerusalem.

Jerusalem was protected by massive walls and defended by a strong, though small, army. The crusaders had little food, no water, and no wood to build siege towers. However, assured of victory by a holy hermit, they attacked on June 13. Their efforts were useless. Four days later, six ships carrying food and wood arrived at Jaffa. Siege towers were hurriedly built and wheeled into position at night. On July 13, a new attack was mounted, and two days later the city was in crusader hands. Terrible scenes followed as the Christians massacred thousands of men, women, and children in a savage frenzy. Neither Jew nor Muslim was left alive.

Emperor Alexius, already angered by the crusaders' failure to return conquered territories, was horrified at their barbarity. The Christian lords did not pause to reflect on their actions. They were wrangling over who should govern Jerusalem. The task fell to Godfrey of Bouillon. When he died in 1100, his brother Baldwin took the title of King, and Jerusalem became the third Crusader State.

THE TAFURS

The Tafurs (from the Arabic for "poor") were Flemish disciples of Peter the Hermit. Like him, they tagged along with the official armies following the collapse of the People's Crusade. Penniless, but full of religious fervor, they urged the lords onward to Jerusalem. Merciless in their attacks on the Turks, they may have joined other crusaders in cannibalism.

The sword and spurs (spikes attached to riding boots) of Crusade leader Godfrey of Bouillon.

Raymond of Aguilers was chaplain to Raymond of Toulouse and witnessed the capture of Jerusalem. In his book *Historia Francorum* (*History of the Franks*), he described the appalling events that took place immediately afterwards.

... Some of our men cut off the heads of their enemies; others shot them with arrows, so that they fell from the towers; others tortured them longer by casting them into the flames. Piles of heads, hands, and feet were to be seen in the streets of the city. It was necessary to pick one's way over the bodies of men and horses. But these were small matters compared to what happened at the temple of Solomon, a place where religious services are ordinarily chanted. ... If I tell the truth, it will exceed your powers of belief. ... in the temple and portico of Solomon, men rode in blood up to their knees and bridle reins. Indeed, it was a just and splendid judgement of God, that this place should be filled with the blood of the unbelievers, when it had suffered so long from their blasphemies ...

A type of porchway.

Actions or words offensive to God.

Until the writer makes this statement, it sounds as if he is criticizing the crusaders. Now it becomes clear that he approves of their actions.

TACTICS AND WEAPONS

Christian and Muslim forces used different battle tactics, weapons, and dress.

On the battlefield, Christian knights relied on brute force. They fought in units called battalions, and their main weapon was the lance. Their stallions could bear the weight of men in metal armor. Knights lowered their lances and rode toward their enemies in a wall. If their lances did not kill, they attacked with swords. The charge technique worked only if the enemy did not simply ride away. The Muslims, who were expert riders, often did.

Crusaders wore a metal helmet, a padded jacket called an aketon, and a chain mail coat called a hauberk. Armor provided some protection against Muslim arrows and swords, but the mail weighed about 30 lb. (13.5 kg). Inside this heavy metal skin, knights broiled under the Middle Eastern sun. They wore a fabric tunic known as a surcoat (see page 19) over the hauberk to reflect the heat away.

Muslim armies depended on mobility rather than strength. Their mares could twist and turn in battle, then race away. In long-range fighting, soldiers used bows and arrows. They could unleash a hail of arrows riding toward the enemy or away. They tried to split the crusaders' battalions, so that soldiers could be tackled individually. (See battle plan, page 45.)

Muslim soldiers used a variety of weapons in hand-to-hand combat, including swords, javelins, lances, and clubs. Some fighters wore leather armor, others no armor at all. They relied on their fighting and riding skills to stay alive.

Women lay siege to a castle in this 13th-century illustration.

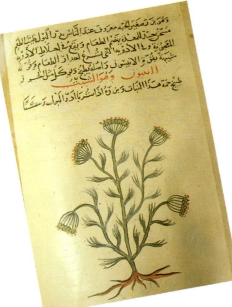

This page comes from an Arabic copy of a work on medicinal plants by early Greek writer Dioscorides. At the time of the crusades, Arab doctors were much more skilled than their European counterparts. So wounded Muslim soldiers often received better care than Christians.

 This is how Anna Comnena (see page 21) described crusader armor in *The Alexiad:*

Ibn Al-Athir (see page 23), described the siege of Acre, in the Third Crusade, 1190. He illustrates some of the problems of siege warfare:

Wooden siege towers often caught fire. Muslim armies under siege pelted the towers with Greek fire, but Christian armies did not then know how to make this substance.

"Greek fire" was a highly flammable mixture of sulfur, naphtha, and other substances. It was placed in clay pots and lit before being thrown.

SIEGE WARFARE

Many battles were won and lost by sieges. These military operations, in which enemy castles and cities were surrounded and cut off from the outside world, had their own specialized equipment.

Siege towers were tall, narrow wooden structures mounted on wheels and moved close to enemy fortifications. At the bottom, each tower housed a massive battering ram. Higher up, archers perched on the platforms that divided the tower into stories, raining arrows down on their opponents. Other useful siege items were scaling ladders and massive machines called mangonels, which hurled heavy stones, or even severed heads, over the walls.

"Crusader."

... **Keltic** armor consists of a tunic interwoven with iron rings linked one with another; the iron is of good quality, capable of resisting an arrow and giving protection to the soldier's body. This armor is supplemented by a shield, not round but long, broad at the top and tapering to a point; inside it is slightly curved; the outside is smooth and shiny, and it has a flashing **bronze boss**. Any arrow... will be repelled by that shield and rebound against the firer...

A small round raised area.

A unit of measurement the length of an adult forearm.

... the Franks built three lofty wooden towers, each one sixty **cubits** tall. They had five floors, each crowded with soldiers. [The towers] were covered with skins, vinegar, mud, and fire-resisting **substances**. The Franks cleared a path for their advance and brought all three up under the walls of Acre ... The fighting lasted for eight days on end ... The Muslims were now convinced that the Franks would take the city ... They had exhausted every stratagem to no avail, and followed this by showering the towers with **Greek fire**, but made no impression ...

THE CRUSADER STATES
OUTREMER

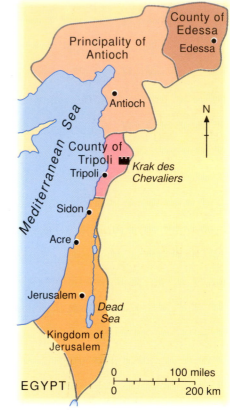

THE CRUSADER STATES

By 1100, the crusaders controlled three states in the Middle East: the County of Edessa, the Principality of Antioch (see pages 22-23), and the Kingdom of Jerusalem (see pages 24-25). Collectively, these were known as Outremer, French for "overseas." Confined to small areas of land and hugely outnumbered by hostile native populations, Europeans in Outremer were vulnerable. The rulers of the Crusader States, particularly King Baldwin I (see page 25) and his successors in Jerusalem, tried to improve their situation.

Baldwin and his fellow princes conquered many Muslim ports, including Acre (1104) and Sidon (1110). They also strengthened their hold on inland areas by winning territory from Egyptians and Turks. In 1109, they completed their conquest of the Muslim emirates separating Antioch from Jerusalem. These new territories formed the fourth Crusader State, the County of Tripoli. To defend their lands and keep a watchful eye on Muslim armies and caravans, the crusaders also created a network of castles, such as Krak des Chevaliers (see map).

When the crusaders first took control in Outremer, they often mistreated their Muslim subjects. However, there were not enough Europeans to cultivate land and organize trade, so they established

The ruins of the mighty Crusader fortress Krak des Chevaliers still stand today.

working relationships with their former enemies. Nevertheless, Muslims, Jews, and Byzantines were made very aware of their inferior status.

To bring order to Outremer, the crusaders introduced feudal government. In Jerusalem, for example, the king granted land to lords in return for military service, and the lords in turn granted land to knights. State affairs were discussed and decided in the High Court, attended by the king, lords, and the masters of the Military Orders (see pages 32-33). Muslims ran local affairs much as they had always done, except that community leaders now had to report to Christian lords and collect taxes on their behalf.

The crusaders promoted Roman Catholicism over other forms of Christianity. In particular, they wanted to end the power of the Greek Orthodox Church in the Holy Land. So they expelled the Patriarchs of Jerusalem and Antioch and replaced them with Roman Catholic bishops.

Fulcher of Chartres, Baldwin I's chaplain (see page 19), made this candid assessment of his master's weak position during his early years as king of Jerusalem.

Also known as Jaffa.

Footsoldiers.

... For we did not at that time have more than three hundred knights and as many footmen to defend Jerusalem, Joppa, Ramla, and also the stronghold of Haifa. We scarcely dared to assemble our knights when we wished to plan some feat against our enemies. We feared that in the meantime they would do some damage against our deserted fortifications...

The Muslims.

AN ILL WIND ...

Godfrey of Bouillon, Jerusalem's first crusader ruler, requested help from Pope Paschal II in 1099. Three armies set out but were slaughtered by the Turks on Byzantine land.

The other way to reach the Holy Land was by sea. More pilgrims and soldiers began to arrive by ship from the Italian ports of Genoa, Venice, and Pisa. These cities had already provided ships, supplies, and military assistance to the crusaders. Now their power was set to increase (see pages 30-31).

LIFE IN OUTREMER

European settlers in Outremer admired many aspects of Arab and Turkish civilization. Middle Eastern customs were far better suited to the climate and conditions than their own, so gradually, they adopted some features of Muslim lifestyles. This was particularly true of second-generation settlers who had been born in Outremer and were known as *pulani* (chickens).

Crusader dress was influenced by Middle Eastern styles. European men began to wear light, flowing robes, open-toed sandals, and sometimes turbans, while women hid their faces behind veils, like their Muslim counterparts. Soldiers exchanged their short military crops for shoulder-length hair. The settlers adopted Eastern standards of cleanliness, too, regularly visiting steam baths and using soap.

Food was another important area in which the conquerors learned from the conquered. Dates, watermelons, lemons, oranges, olives, and sugarcane were new to the settlers. The crusaders learned to mix fruits with mountain snow to make sorbets. They flavored their food with spices such as pepper, cinnamon, and ginger, which were imported from India and China and widely available in the Middle East.

Rich crusader settlers often lived in grander mansions than they might have possessed at home. They covered the floors with woven carpets and the walls with fine silk hangings. They ate from gold and silver plates on carved tables. They also created Islamic-style gardens, whose fountains and greenery provided shelter from the heat of the sun.

There were many pastimes to enjoy in the Middle East. Men went hunting with hawks for deer and hare. (This could be dangerous—King Fulk of Jerusalem died when he fell from his horse during a hunt.) They also listened to music and played on instruments such as lutes and drums. Some people learned to play chess.

Most of these novelties affected Europeans living not only in the Middle East but in Europe itself. For as crusaders returned home, they took their new ideas with them. Soon the crusader influence was felt in areas of life as far removed from warfare as food and fashion.

TRADING PROFITS

Trade as well as passenger transport between Outremer and Europe was organized through the Italian ports of Genoa, Venice, and Pisa. Antioch, Beirut, and Acre became important centers for commerce between East and West.

The Italians won the right to deal in commodities including sugar, silk, and spices. They had to pay a tax to the king of Jerusalem of 10 percent of the goods' value, but they still made huge profits and became very wealthy.

The waters of the Mediterranean Sea still lap the 12th-century walls of Acre today. Since 1948, the city has been part of Israel.

Usama ibn Munqidh was one of the emirs of Syria. He met many influential Syrians, Egyptians, and crusaders during a long, eventful life (1095–1188). His autobiography, *Kitab al-Itibar (Book of Instruction with Illustrations)*, tells how some crusaders followed Islamic dietary laws.

A crusader.

... One day [the Governor of Antioch] said to my friend: "A Frankish friend has invited me to visit him; come with me so you can see how they live." "I went with him," said my friend, "and we came to the house of one of the old knights who came with the first expedition ... He had a fine table brought out, spread with a splendid selection of appetizing food. He saw that I was not eating, and said: 'Don't worry, please; eat what you like, for I don't eat Frankish food. I have Egyptian cooks and eat only what they serve. No pig's flesh ever comes into my house!'" ...

An original page of Arabic script from Usama ibn Munqidh's book.

Islam forbids the eating of pork.

Fulcher of Chartres (see pages 19 and 29) described the ways in which many Europeans adapted to living in the Middle East.

People from the West.

Been baptized as Christians.

Muslims.

Many different.

... 3. For we who were Occidentals have now become Orientals... We have already forgotten the places of our birth;...

4. Some already possess homes or households by inheritance. Some have taken ... Syrians or Armenians or even Saracens [as wives] who have obtained the grace of baptism...

5. People use ... diverse languages in conversing back and forth. Words of different languages have become property known to each nationality, and mutual faith unites those who are ignorant of their descent. ...

THE MILITARY ORDERS

Two orders of soldier monks dedicated themselves to the struggle for the Holy Land. Crusader rulers valued them, since they were the only permanent Christian armies in the Middle East.

About 1070, merchants from Amalfi in Italy set up the Hospital of St. John in Jerusalem to care for Christian pilgrims, especially the sick. In 1113, the Pope recognized the monks who ran the hospital as an independent religious order. Raymond du Puy, the order's second Master, turned the monks into a fighting order, called Knights Hospitaller, after the Hospital of St. John.

The second military order was founded in 1119 by French knight Hugh of Payens and eight others. Their headquarters were at the royal palace in Jerusalem. As this was near the supposed site of the Temple of Solomon (see page 12), the men called themselves Knights Templar. Like the Hospitallers, the Templars took vows of poverty, chastity, and obedience. Their first duty was to protect the pilgrim route from the coast to Jerusalem, but they soon took on a broader military role.

These military orders attracted donations from the pious, including estates in many countries that brought substantial incomes. Their prestige ensured recruits from the noble families of Europe. Rich and independent—they were answerable only to the Pope—they managed crusader castles, organized armies for crusader rulers, and lent kings money to wage war.

The Hospitallers still exist, though in a different form (see page 57). But Philip IV of France arrested all the French Templars in 1307, and the order was

The painful death suffered by many Knights Templar in the early 14th century is shown in this illustration from the period.

A meeting of the Knights Templar in Paris in 1147. The participants are wearing the order's trademark white tunics marked with red crosses. The painting is by French artist Marius Granet (1775–1849).

abolished in 1312. At the time, its members were accused of crimes against Christianity, and many were burned at the stake. Some historians think that Philip genuinely believed they were guilty. Others think that he resented their power and needed their money.

The original document of the Chippenham land grant (see below).

The address given to those wishing to join the Knights Hospitaller made clear that there was no easy life ahead:

... when you would desire to eat, it will be necessary for you to fast, and when you would wish to fast, you will have to eat. And when you would desire to sleep, it will be necessary for you to keep watch, and when you would like to ... watch, you will have to sleep. And you will be sent this side of the sea and beyond ... and you will have to go there. It will be necessary for you ... to endure other hardships in the Order, more than I can describe ...

THE TEUTONIC KNIGHTS

In 1190, during the Third Crusade (see pages 46-47), German merchants set up a hospital in Acre. In 1191, the monks there were recognized as a new religious order, and in 1198 they became a fighting order, the Teutonic Knights. These military monks, who were all members of the German aristocracy, fought for the Holy Land until Christians were expelled in 1291. By that time they had another power base in northern Europe, around the Baltic Sea. From there, they organized violent crusades against Prussians, Lithuanians, and other pagan peoples (see pages 52-53).

Around 1280, a man granted land in Chippenham, Cambridgeshire, to the Knights Hospitaller:

People hoped that God would allow them into heaven if they gave away land and property to the military orders.

...Thomas le Merveillus [the Marvellous] of Dalham grants to God, Blessed Mary and St John the Baptist and the blessed poor of the house of the Hospital of Jerusalem and to the brethren of the same house dwelling together at Chippenham and serving God there, for the salvation of my soul and the souls of my ancestors and descendants, sixty acres of ... land in the fields of Ashley and Silverley ...

THE MUSLIMS FIGHT BACK
A DIVIDED WORLD

The loss of Jerusalem (see pages 24-25) was a devastating blow to the Muslims, but they failed to fight back effectively for some years. The Turks were not only at odds with the Egyptians but also divided among themselves. Rival emirs fought endlessly, while the sons of Malik Shah (see pages 16-17) engaged in a family struggle to succeed him.

However, as the crusaders continued to extend their territories (see pages 28-29), Muslims realized that they must unite or face further losses. In 1110, the Turkish Sultan

Minarets rise above the crowded streets of Damascus in Syria.

Mohammed asked Mawdud, the Emir of Mosul, to lead a joint Muslim assault on the crusaders in Edessa. Although they were not able to capture the state, Mawdud's forces slaughtered many Christian civilians. Later Muslim attacks on Aleppo and Damascus also had limited success, but the tide had begun to turn. Mawdud's career ended in 1113 when he was killed by an assassin (see page 17), but by then, another Muslim leader was emerging.

The new leader was Ilghazi, a gifted but unorthodox general who had fought with Mawdud against the Christians. In 1118, the inhabitants of Aleppo asked him to become ruler of their city, which many Turkish and crusader leaders had long battled to win. Now it was under threat from a

Crusaders and Muslims fight hand to hand in this grim scene, while their horses die unnoticed.

Christian prince, Roger of Antioch. On June 28, 1119, Ilghazi and his army surrounded Roger's forces as they slept. A disastrous defeat followed for the Christians. Roger and most of his men were killed, and the few survivors were tortured. The terrible loss of life led the crusaders to christen the battlefield *Ager Sanguinis*, Latin for "Field of Blood."

Ilghazi failed to build on his great victory and was soon driven back by King Baldwin II of Jerusalem. After Ilghazi's death, his nephew Balak regained some former Muslim territory and even managed to imprison Baldwin himself. Balak never had the chance to become the great leader the Muslims needed. In 1124 he was killed during a siege, and the Christians were again free to continue their conquests. But not for long.

 The following two accounts describe the horrific "Field of Blood." Walter, Roger of Antioch's chancellor, gives a Christian viewpoint. The Muslim account was written later by Kamal ad-Din, who produced two histories of Aleppo, the city where he was born in A.D. 1192.

JIHAD

Muslim refugees from the carnage in Jerusalem and from other conquered territories fled to Aleppo (below) and Damascus. There they encouraged Turkish rulers and Arab subjects alike to wage a holy war, or *jihad* (see page 11), against the Christians. From this time on *jihad* helped unite Muslims against their common enemy and inspired them to reclaim their lands.

... Suddenly the flags and standards of the heathens appeared from the mountainsides among the olives... Prince Roger declared: "Soldiers of Christ, ... let us ...serve today as soldiers for God in a successful battle, whether we end up alive or dead."

Prince Roger engaged in the struggle with steadfast mind. Although his men lay cut down and dead on all sides, he never retreated or looked back, but ... obeyed the command of God ... by fighting energetically against the force of the entire military might... [Walter]

... God gave victory to the Muslims. The Franks who fled to their camp were slaughtered. The Turks fought superbly... Arrows flew thick as locusts, and the Franks, with missiles raining down on infantry and cavalry alike, turned and fled. The cavalry was destroyed, the infantry cut to pieces, the followers and servants were all taken prisoner. Roger was killed but [only] twenty Muslims were lost ... whereas only twenty Franks escaped. A few of the leaders got away, but almost 15,000 men fell in the battle ... [Kamal ad-Din]

THE FALL OF EDESSA

Another skillful warrior, Imad ed-Din Zengi, came to the rescue after Balak's death. He restored shattered Muslim pride, dealing a mighty blow to the Christians by capturing a Crusader State.

Imad ed-Din Zengi was a rough, straight-talking soldier with a forceful personality. In 1127, he became Emir of Mosul, and a year later took over Aleppo. Then he set out to expand his territory. Zengi's motives were mixed. He had a deep-rooted wish to expel the crusaders by waging holy war against them. But at the same time, he was hungry for power over as large an area as possible. So he captured lands from Turks as well as Christians, tackling his Turkish rivals first. By 1135, Zengi controlled a string of towns in Iraq and Syria.

Zengi's first major strike against the Christians took place in 1137, when he defeated the forces of King Fulk of Jerusalem. Then a strange alliance was made.

Zengi had been unable to capture Damascus in Syria from its Muslim governor, Unur. After his success against the crusaders he decided to try again, and in 1140 besieged the city. The city's inhabitants turned not to fellow Muslims but to the crusaders of Jerusalem for support. In June 1140, Christian forces led by King Fulk joined Muslim forces led by Unur to form a massive army. There was no battle. Zengi realized that he had been outmaneuvred and retreated to Aleppo with his troops.

The marriage of Fulk of Anjou to Melisende of Jerusalem.

Zengi's next act of aggression was much more successful. In 1144, he attacked an ally of Joscelin, Count of the Crusader State of Edessa. Joscelin promptly went to his ally's aid, leaving Edessa largely undefended. Zengi then besieged Edessa for four weeks. Edessa's fortifications were strong, so the besieging soldiers tunnelled underneath them. On Christmas Eve, Zengi ordered his men to set fire to the wooden tunnel supports. The city walls above collapsed and soldiers rushed in. The state had fallen.

The Islamic world rejoiced at this new turn of events. But the Christian world recoiled in horror. Something would have to be done.

THE DEATH OF ZENGI

Following his great victory in Edessa, Zengi became a hero. He continued his campaigns for two more years, but was still unable to take Damascus. In 1146, he set out on yet another expedition to capture the city. On the way, he shouted at one of his slaves, who had dared to drink from his master's cup. The slave had his revenge. During the night of September 14, he waited until Zengi fell asleep. Then he stabbed him to death in his bed.

Ibn Al-Athir (see page 23) was a great supporter of Zengi, and always emphasized his virtues, as in this account:

... Zengi was a handsome man, with a swarthy complexion, fine eyes, and hair that was beginning to go gray. He was more than sixty years old, ... His subjects and his army went in awe of him; under his government the strong dared not harm the weak. Before he came to power, the absence of strong rulers to impose justice, and the presence of the Franks close at hand, had made the country a wilderness, but he made it flower again...

Michael the Syrian, a Christian Jacobite (died 1199), recorded the Fall of Edessa in his *Chronicle*. Zengi allowed only Roman Catholic Christians to be massacred at Edessa, because he regarded them as Muslims' particular enemies. Soon after the events described here, he stepped in to prevent the slaughter of Greek Orthodox, Jacobite, and other Eastern Christians.

... Edessa was trampled underfoot...the priests massacred, the deacons sacrificed, and their assistants beaten to death, the churches ransacked and the altars thrown to the ground. Alas, what a calamity! Fathers denied their sons, mothers forgot the love they bore their children! As the swords cut them down, many fled to the mountaintop, some gathered their children around them as a hen gathers her chicks, and waited huddled together to die by the sword or be taken into captivity ...

Roman Catholic ministers who were less important than a priest.

THE SECOND CRUSADE

Stunned by events in Edessa, the crusaders appealed to Pope Eugenius III for help. Eugenius then called on Louis VII of France to lead an army to the Holy Land. Louis enlisted the help of a famous preacher, Bernard of Clairvaux, Abbot of the Cistercian order (see page 15). On March 31, 1146, Bernard preached at Vézélay in France. After his sermon, hundreds of people took the cross eagerly. The Second Crusade was under way.

The German king, Conrad III, also joined the crusade. In May 1147 his armies took the land route to Constantinople, then crossed into Asia, where they were attacked by a vast Seljuk army. Conrad was among the few crusaders to survive.

The French reached Constantinople in early October. They met the remains of Conrad's army, and the combined forces made their way east.

At Antioch, Raymond, its ruler, tried to persuade Louis to join an attack against Nur ed-Din (see pages 40-41). The king refused, determined to press on to Jerusalem.

Louis and Conrad attended a grand meeting in Acre arranged by King Baldwin III of Jerusalem. They agreed with the local princes to attack Damascus—the only friendly Muslim city in the region. When the crusaders rode into battle in May 1148, they failed to take the city. Defeated and depressed, Louis and Conrad returned to Europe.

At the Council of Acre (left, top), the Christian kings Baldwin, Conrad, and Louis agreed to besiege the Muslim city of Damascus (left, bottom).

ELEANOR OF AQUITAINE

At Vézélay, Eleanor of Aquitaine took the cross along with her husband King Louis VII (right). Many noblewomen followed. Some people praised their piety, others accused them of distracting men from serious crusading.

Eleanor was accused of having an affair with Raymond, her uncle, while at Antioch. She certainly supported his plan to attack Nur ed-Din against her husband's wishes. Louis left for Jerusalem, forcing Eleanor to go with him. Eleanor and Louis had also failed to produce a male heir, and on their return to France in 1152, they were divorced. In 1154, Eleanor married Henry II of England and became the mother of Richard I (see pages 46-47).

Odo of Deuil was Louis VII's chaplain during the Second Crusade. In his book, *The Journey of Louis VII to the East*, he describes the extraordinary events in Vézélay when Bernard of Clairvaux preached there in 1146.

A page from Odo's book, which was written in Latin.

Bernard, speaking as inspired by God.

... since there was no place within the town which could accommodate such a large crowd, a wooden platform was erected outside in a field ... [Bernard] mounted the platform accompanied by the king, who was wearing the cross; and when **heaven's instrument** poured forth the dew of the divine word ... with loud outcry people on every side began to demand crosses. And when he had **sowed** ... the parcel of crosses which had been prepared beforehand, he was forced to tear his own garments into crosses and to sow them abroad...

Bernard had to throw them into the crowd like seed rather than hand them out.

In his history, William of Tyre, chancellor of Jerusalem during the reign of Baldwin IV (1174–1185), describes the attack on Damascus. The crusaders began well, but for unknown reasons they left their strong position in the orchards and lost the battle.

... All the military strength of the realm was therefore assembled, both horsemen and foot-soldiers, natives, and pilgrims ... on May, 25 1148, the combined forces [Louis and Conrad], with the cross of salvation at their head, marched ... they decided that the best way to lay siege to the city was to start by seizing the orchards which surrounded most of Damascus and gave it a great deal of protection Once these had been captured there was no doubt that Damascus itself could be seized with ease...

SYRIA UNITED

After the death of Zengi, his son, Nur ed-Din, became the champion of Islam. Unlike Zengi, Nur ed-Din was a pious Muslim, but he was just as good as Zengi in a fight.

Nur ed-Din was committed to *jihad* and the recapture of Jerusalem. However, as Emir of Aleppo, he first set out to finish the work his father had begun of unifying Syria. In June 1149, his troops almost wiped out the armies of Raymond of Antioch and killed Raymond himself (see page 38). Nur ed-Din put Raymond's skull in a silver casket and sent it to the Caliph of Baghdad as a trophy.

Many other cities fell before Nur ed-Din's advancing armies. By 1154, he was ready to tackle the greatest Syrian prize, Damascus. In April, his troops camped outside the city. Its citizens, short of food and unhappy with their own ruler, soon opened the gates to the army. Syria was again strong and united, while the Crusader States were weak and divided.

Nur ed-Din proved to be an inspired ruler. He set up a fair system of taxes and an efficient administration, with a governor in each region and a judge in each major city. He built hospitals, public baths, and in Damascus even a hippodrome for horse racing. He also constructed numerous mosques (see box). Although an austere man who personally spent little money, he built a new residence, the Golden Palace in Damascus, where he kept a magnificent court.

Nur ed-Din knew the value of propaganda. He

The city of Damascus today.

employed people to write songs, poems, and speeches describing what an excellent ruler he was and what a stout defender of Islam. Couriers had for a long time traveled by horse and camel carrying documents between governors, but Nur ed-Din introduced a new, quicker means of relaying messages—carrier pigeons. This was just as efficient in war as it was in everyday life.

Under Nur ed-Din, Syria prospered. But there were still battles to be fought for Islam, and the new battleground was Egypt.

MOSQUES, *MADRASAS*, AND *KHANQAS*

Nur ed-Din promoted Sunni Islam. He built many mosques and increased the number of religious schools, known as *madrasas*, from 16 to 58. Religious institutions called *khanqas* also flourished, where followers of Sufism, a mystical branch of Islam, studied and worshiped. The Sufis played a significant role in the *jihad* against Christians. But they also preached the importance of waging *jihad* against one's own sins.

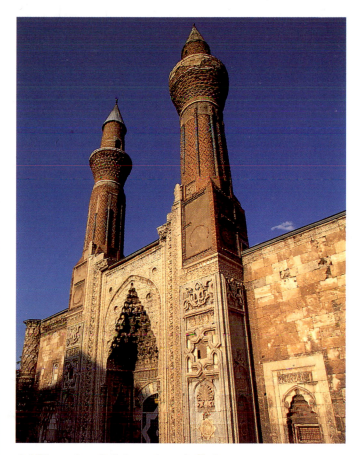

A 13th-century Seljuk *madrasa* in Turkey.

 This is how Ibn Al-Athir (see page 23) described Nur ed-Din.

... Among his virtues were austerity, piety, and a knowledge of theology. His food and clothing and all his personal expenditure came out of income from properties bought with his legal share of booty and money allocated for communal Muslim interests ... He had a good knowledge of Muslim law... but he was not a fanatic ... On the battlefield he had no equal; he carried two bows and quivers into the fray with him ... Among his public works he built walls for all the cities and fortresses of Syria...

 Abu Shama, a teacher born in Damascus in 1203, compiled the anthology *Kitab ar-Raudatain (The Book of the Two Gardens)*. Here he describes Nur ed-Din's use of carrier pigeons:

... In the year 1171, Nur ed-Din gave orders to use carrier pigeons. These are the messenger birds that fly back to their lofts from distant lands. They were adopted in all his territories ... On the borders of his lands he had men on duty with pigeons ... When they saw or heard anything, they at once wrote it down, attached it to the bird, and sent it off without delay...

THE THIRD AND FOURTH CRUSADES
THE RISE OF SALADIN

In 1162, Amalric came to power in Jerusalem. He had to act against Nur ed-Din's Syria, to the north, to prevent the powerful Muslim ruler from taking over Fatimid Egypt, to the south. Otherwise, surrounded by one united body of Muslims, his kingdom would fall. However, Amalric's first attempt at invasion, in 1163, was a failure.

A year later, an Egyptian vizier, Shawar, asked Nur ed-Din to overthrow the Shi'ite rulers of Egypt and replace them with a Sunni government led by Shawar himself. In return, Shawar would recognize Nur ed-Din as his overlord and give him land and money. Nur ed-Din agreed, and sent an army led by a gifted Kurdish general called Shirkuh. With Shirkuh went his young nephew Saladin.

Shirkuh defeated the Egyptians easily and in May 1164, Shawar returned to Cairo in triumph. He then broke the promises he had made and commanded Shirkuh to leave. Shirkuh refused, so Shawar turned to Amalric for help. The king intervened, and Shirkuh was forced out.

Encouraged by their success, in 1168 the crusaders made a pact with the Byzantines to conquer Egypt. The crusader army set out in October 1168. When they arrived in the Egyptian town of Bilbeis, Shawar was astonished. He had thought that the crusaders were still on his side. When they massacred the city's inhabitants and went on to besiege Cairo, he realized his position was hopeless. So he shamelessly turned back to Nur ed-Din and Shirkuh for help.

Shirkuh, Saladin, and an army that included 8,000 cavalry, hurriedly set out for Egypt. Outnumbered and also outmaneuvered, the crusaders retreated. Shirkuh pushed onward and on January 8, 1169, entered Cairo. Ten days later, Shawar was assassinated by Saladin and a group of colleagues, and Shirkuh became the new vizier.

This portrait of Saladin was painted during his lifetime by a Muslim artist. It is the most realistic picture existing of this great leader.

When he died in March, of overeating, Saladin took his place and later became Sultan of Egypt. When Nur ed-Din died in 1174, his son was only ten, so Saladin returned to Damascus and took over his former master's role there, too.

Flocks of sheep and their shepherds still roam the ancient lands of the Kurds today.

THE KURDS

Shirkuh, Saladin, and many other soldiers in the armies of Nur ed-Din were Kurds. Most Kurds were poor farmers and shepherds in northern Iraq, western Iran, and eastern Anatolia (present-day Turkey). Before the Seljuks invaded, they had established small Muslim states, ruled by princes. They lost much of their territory to the Turks and accepted them as rulers. Zengi (see pages 36–37) was the first Turk actively to recruit Kurds for his armies, a practice continued by Nur ed-Din.

In the 13th century, an anonymous canon of a London church wrote a book about King Richard I (see pages 46-47) called *Itinerarium regis Ricardi*. It included a highly critical account of Saladin's early life.

The anglicized form of "Yusuf" (see below).

... Saladin, this great persecutor of Christianity, ... was of Kurdish stock, and his parents were not noble. However, in spite of this lowly beginning, his life did not follow the pattern of common folk. His father's name was Job, and he himself was known as Joseph... He was inspired with hopes of the kingdom by the prophecy of a certain Syrian, who foretold that he would hold sway over Damascus and Cairo. So he began to aspire to greater things than the kingdom beyond whose narrow limits and boundaries he had never gone...

According to Saladin's own account, he was reluctant to leave Syria for Egypt:

... My uncle Shirkuh turned to me and said: "Yusuf, pack your things, we're going." When I heard this order, I felt as if my heart had been pierced by a dagger, and I answered, "In God's name, even were I granted the entire kingdom of Egypt, I would not go." In the end I did go with my uncle. He conquered Egypt, then died. God then placed in my hands power that I had never expected...

THE RECAPTURE OF JERUSALEM

Saladin was committed to *jihad* and the recapture of Jerusalem from the Christians, but he also had Turkish opponents in cities such as Aleppo and Mosul. They believed that Saladin was too lowly to rule over them, and that Nur ed-Din's young son, as-Salih, was the rightful heir.

Saladin fought Christians and Turks alike. In 1183 he conquered Aleppo, uniting Syria and Egypt under his control and trapping the Crusader States inside his territories. The Christians had other problems, too. In 1185, King Baldwin IV of Jerusalem died of leprosy. His heir, Baldwin V, died a year later, plunging Jerusalem into dispute over the succession. Guy of Lusignan was crowned, but he was no match for Saladin.

Saladin leads his troops into Jerusalem to reclaim it for the Muslims.

This 15th-century image of Saladin comes from an Italian book about famous people in world history.

Reynald of Châtillon brought on the inevitable conflict. A knight who had arrived in the Holy Land during the Second Crusade, he had long taunted Saladin and provoked the Muslim ruler's hatred. At the end of 1186, Reynald broke a truce by attacking a Muslim caravan on the way from Cairo to Damascus. In 1187, Saladin assembled the greatest army he had ever commanded, around 60,000 men, and set out to confront the Christians.

The great clash took place in searing heat beneath a hill with twin peaks known as the Horns of Hattin. The only well in the area was dry, and to add to the Christians' thirst, Saladin lit fires around their camp. During the night of July 3-4, 1187, the Muslim forces surrounded the weak, water-starved army. The battle began at dawn, and the knights and foot soldiers of Jerusalem were all but wiped out. Those who survived, including King Guy, were taken prisoner.

The Kingdom of Jerusalem was now at Saladin's mercy. He moved across the land, conquering its cities one by one. Finally, on October 2, 1187, he entered Jerusalem itself. Almost ninety years of Christian rule in the city had come to an end.

THE TRUE CROSS

The Bishop of Acre had carried a precious Christian relic into the Battle of Hattin. This was believed to be a piece of the True Cross on which Jesus Christ was crucified. During the fighting, the bishop was killed and the holy relic fell into Muslim hands. The Christians saw this as an omen of disaster and sank into great despair.

Imad ad-Din was Saladin's chancellor and secretary. He wrote a history of his master's recapture of Jerusalem, and here he describes the scene after the Battle of Hattin.

A battle plan showing troop positions from one of Saladin's manuals.

... of all those enemies only a few were saved. The plain was covered with prisoners and corpses, disclosed by the dust as it settled and victory became clear. The prisoners, with beating hearts, were bound in chains. The dead were scattered over the mountains and valleys, lying immobile on their sides. Hattin shrugged off their carcasses, and the perfume of victory was thick with the stench of them...

Here Ibn Al-Athir (see page 23) tells of the efforts of Muslims to cleanse their holy shrines once they had recaptured Jerusalem.

Arabic, meaning "God is great."

The name of a mosque.

... At the top of the cupola of the Dome of the Rock there was a great gilded cross. When the Muslims entered the city on the Friday, some of them climbed to the top of the cupola to take down the cross... a great cry went up from the city and from outside the walls, the Muslims crying **"Allah akbar"** in their joy, the Franks groaning in consternation and grief. So loud and piercing was the cry that the earth shook.

... Saladin ordered that the shrines should be restored to their original state. The Templars had built their living-quarters against **al-Aqsa**, with storerooms and latrines ... This was all restored to its former state. The Sultan ordered that the Dome of the Rock should be cleansed of all pollution, and this was done...

THE THIRD CRUSADE

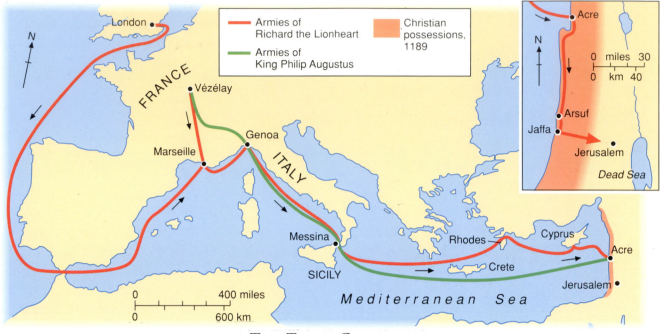

Armies of Richard the Lionheart
Armies of King Philip Augustus
Christian possessions, 1189

THE THIRD CRUSADE

When the news of Jerusalem's fall reached Pope Gregory VIII, he appealed for a third crusade to restore the city to the Christians. Three rulers were to head the avenging armies: Philip Augustus of France, Richard I of England (Richard the Lionheart), and Emperor Frederick Barbarossa of Germany. However, Frederick drowned on the way across Anatolia in 1189. Richard and Philip set out from France in 1190, aiming to meet at Messina in Sicily before continuing to the Holy Land.

Richard's fleet was delayed, so he arrived in Sicily late. Winter was coming and the weather was too bad to travel east by sea, so the crusaders had to wait on the island until spring. Finally, in March 1191, Philip set sail. Richard's fleet was caught in a storm, and he had to make a detour to collect his shipwrecked mother and his wife-to-be, Berengaria, in Cyprus. While there, he conquered the island.

The kings' destination in the Holy Land was the important trading port of Acre (see page 30), where a siege had been in progress for two years. Inside the city were its Muslim rulers. Outside were Christians led by Guy of Lusignan (whom Saladin had freed) and Conrad of Montferrat. Beyond them were Saladin's forces, who launched frequent attacks. When Philip arrived in April 1191, he helped the Christians to build new siege engines, including a catapult called "God's Own Sling." When Richard arrived with twenty-five war galleys in June, he provided the leadership that the Christians needed to take the city. On July 11, Acre surrendered. Saladin had suffered a serious defeat.

King Philip and his troops at Acre during the Third Crusade.

WOMEN AT WAR

Richard did not welcome women on crusade. He tolerated those who tagged along to do the washing or pick the fleas from his soldiers' skin and hair, but he did not want them as fighters. However, he had failed to consider female courage and determination. Several writers record the active part that women played in the Third Crusade as shown below.

 Imad ad-Din (see page 45) describes how women took part in the Third Crusade. He clearly did not approve, but thought their conduct would help the Muslims to win.

Armor that protects the chest and back.

... Among the Franks there were indeed women who rode into battle with **cuirasses** and helmets, dressed in men's clothes; who rode into the thick of the fray and acted like brave men although they were but tender women, maintaining that all this was an act of piety, thinking to gain heavenly rewards by it, and making it their way of life. Praise be to him who led them into such error and out of the paths of wisdom! On the day of battle more than one woman rode out with them like a knight and showed [masculine] endurance in spite of the weakness [of her sex]; clothed only in a coat of mail they were not recognized as women until they had been stripped of their arms ...

 The History of the Holy War by Ambroise explains how King Richard conducted the siege of Acre from his sickbed. He, like Philip, was suffering from a fever called arnaldia. Its unpleasant effects include hair and nail loss.

... From his bed he shot many of the enemy by his own skill with the **arbalest**. In addition his **sappers** carried a mine under the tower, filled it with logs of wood and set them on fire. A **trebuchet** also hurled frequent blows at the tower, a part of which collapsed with a great crash ...Then Richard offered four gold pieces for each stone removed...

A type of large crossbow.

Engineers.

A giant catapult used for throwing rocks.

THE MARCH TO JERUSALEM

After Acre fell, King Philip went home, but Richard had set his heart on recapturing Jerusalem.

Richard left Acre for the Holy City in August 1191, leading his armies down the coast toward Jaffa. His ships sailed alongside carrying supplies and baggage. On September 7, Saladin launched a full-scale attack outside the town of Arsuf, but was forced to retreat. When Richard's troops finally reached Jaffa, they took the city easily.

Richard was a realistic man who knew that the conquest of Jerusalem, a strongly fortified city far inland, was a difficult task. He tried to negotiate with Saladin, who refused to meet him, but sent his brother, al-Adil. The two men could not agree, and battle seemed inevitable.

In December 1191, Richard led his army toward the Holy City, but stopped 12 mi (20 km) from his goal. He had misgivings about holding the city, once it was in Christian hands. He was also worried about his ships while the army was occupied inland. Reluctantly, he turned back to Jaffa, determined to negotiate a solution.

In 1192, Richard's worries deepened when he heard that his brother John was trying to take over in England. He also knew that Philip was threatening his lands in France.

This 12th-century illustration shows (top) the capture of Richard I on his way home across Europe and (bottom) kneeling in front of his final captor, Emperor Henry VI.

How an artist imagined Richard I (below, left) and Saladin in combat.

In June, Richard made one last march on Jerusalem to encourage Saladin to compromise. Meanwhile, Saladin seized Jaffa. Richard hurriedly returned to recapture it. Both ill and weary of conflict, Richard and Saladin signed a three-year truce in September 1192. In October, Richard sailed for home. Five months later, Saladin was dead.

On his way back across Europe, Richard was captured by Leopold of Austria, whom he had offended at Acre by throwing his standard into a moat. Leopold sold him on to Emperor Henry VI. Richard was finally released in February 1194 after a vast ransom had been paid. He then devoted himself to winning back the English lands that Philip had seized during his absence. In 1199, Richard was injured in France during a siege, and on April 6 he died of his wound.

Baha ad-Din, one of Saladin's officials, wrote his biography. In English, this book is called *Sultanly Anecdotes and Josephly Virtues* (Joseph was Saladin's first name, see pages 42-43). The author flatters his master, but is honest. He supports the view, shared by many crusaders, that Saladin was an honorable man.

Saladin's tomb in Damascus, Syria, where he died in 1193.

... Everyone who appeared before him was treated with honor, even an infidel ... Once a Frankish prisoner was brought before him in whom the Sultan aroused such fear that the marks of terror and agitation were visible in his face. The interpreter asked him: "What are you afraid of?" God inspired him to reply: "At first I was afraid of seeing that face, but after seeing it and standing in his presence, I am sure that I shall see only good in it." The Sultan was moved, pardoned him, and let him go free...

This excerpt from the *Itinerarium Regis Ricardi* (see pages 42-43) shows Richard I's great sorrow at his failure to recapture Jerusalem. It describes his emotions as he left the Holy Land.

... All night they sailed by the stars, and as the next day dawned, King Richard gazed back ... Many heard him as he uttered this prayer: "Oh Holy Land, I leave you in God's keeping. May he in his grace grant me length of days that at his good pleasure I may sometime bring unto you the succor that is in my heart" ...

Help.

THE FOURTH CRUSADE

After Richard's failure to reclaim Jerusalem, the crusading spirit faded. In 1198 an ambitious new pope, Innocent III, took office, and decided that the time was right for another crusade.

Innocent recruited a preacher called Fulk of Neuilly. It proved easy to attract the poor, but the rich were harder to persuade. However, in 1199 Theobald, Count of Champagne, and Louis, Count of Blois, agreed to lead the Fourth Crusade. They were joined by Count Baldwin of Flanders. In 1201, Theobald died and was replaced by Boniface, Marquis of Montferrat. The leaders decided to travel by sea from Venice.

The Venetians agreed to build ships to transport 4,500 knights and about 30,000 other soldiers for 85,000 silver marks. They also offered 50 galleys of their own in return for half the crusaders' conquests.

A 13th-century fresco showing Pope Innocent III

The date for completion of the fleet was June 1202. By then, about 20,000 fewer crusaders than expected had arrived in Venice. As the ships were to be paid for by collecting a sum of silver from each participant, the leaders faced a huge debt. But the Venetians were prepared to bargain.

In return for allowing the crusaders to postpone payment, they asked for help in recapturing Zara, a port they had lost to King Emeric of Hungary. The crusaders agreed, even though Emeric was

THE DOGE OF VENICE

The people of Venice elected their ruler, known as the doge, from the Latin *dux*, "leader." At the time of the Fourth Crusade, the Doge of Venice was Enrico Dandolo. He detested the Byzantines because they had given trading rights to Venice's rivals, Pisa and Genoa. So he was glad to join an attack on Constantinople and to take his share of its treasures.

The four horses that adorn St. Mark's Cathedral in Venice were stolen from Constantinople during the sack of the city.

a Christian. The Pope forbade this, but the crusaders ignored him. In 1202, they conquered the port, but did not seize enough booty to repay their debt.

Then another scheme was suggested. In 1201, the Byzantine emperor Isaac Angelus had been deposed. His son, Alexius, promised the crusaders money if they would attack his enemies in Constantinople. He also promised that Byzantium would accept the authority of Rome. The Pope again objected, but the crusaders went ahead.

In 1203, Alexius was made emperor and failed to repay his debts. Then he was murdered, and his successor would not pay either. In 1204, the crusaders sacked Constantinople, killing and looting for three days. The emperor went into exile, and Byzantium was divided between crusaders and Venetians. The Fourth Crusade against Muslims had instead destroyed a Christian empire.

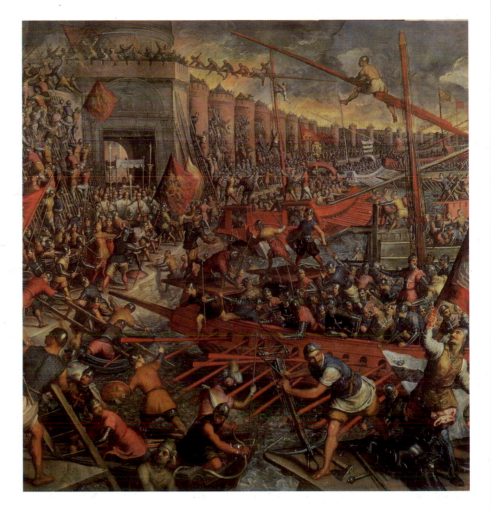

A painting of the sack of Constantinople, by the famous 16th-century Italian artist Tintoretto.

 Geoffrey de Villehardouin was a French noble who accompanied the Fourth Crusade. He later wrote an account called *The Conquest of Constantinople*. Here he describes the sack of Constantinople in 1204.

Ermine and miniver are both types of fur.

... The rest of the army ... gained much booty; ... It included gold and silver, table-services, and precious stones, satin, and silk, mantles of squirrel fur, ermine and miniver, and every choicest thing to be found on this earth. Geoffrey de Villehardouin here declares that, to his knowledge, so much booty had never been gained in any city since the creation of the world.

Everyone took quarters where he pleased, and there was no lack of fine dwellings in that city ... They all rejoiced and gave thanks to our Lord for the honor and the victory he had granted them, so that those who had been poor now lived in wealth and luxury. Thus they celebrated Palm Sunday and the Easter Day following, with hearts full of joy for the benefits our Lord and Savior had bestowed on them ...

THE LATER CRUSADES

THE CATHAR AND BALTIC CRUSADES

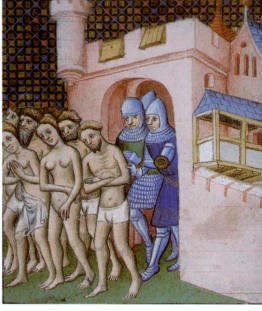

Crusaders throw the inhabitants out of the French city of Carcassonne.

Pope Innocent III also organized crusades against Christians who did not agree with Roman Catholic teachings. Chief among these were the Cathars, also known as Albigensians because one of their strongholds was the town of Albi in Languedoc in southern France.

Cathars believed that two forces were at war in the world; a good, spiritual force and an evil, material force. All matter, including the human body, was therefore evil. The Catholic Church regarded this as heretical, because it denied that God was all-powerful.

Around the centers of Catharism, Toulouse, and Carcassonne, people deserted the Catholic Church. The Bishop of Albi once preached to an empty cathedral. Then, in 1208, the Pope's legate (representative) in Languedoc was murdered, and Innocent declared a crusade against the heretics. He offered forgiveness of sins to anyone who participated.

Crusading armies reached Languedoc in 1209, and Cathars were massacred, but not suppressed. In 1233, Pope Gregory IX set up a series of inquiries, or inquisitions, and commissioned mostly Dominican friars to run it. Some Cathars were tortured to obtain confessions or burned to death for the good of their souls. By the mid-14th century there were few Cathars left.

Pope Innocent also organized the Baltic Crusade, established in 1199. It aimed to support the Roman Catholic Church in Livonia (modern Estonia, Lithuania, and Latvia) and to conquer and convert its pagan enemies. In 1202, a military order of German knights known as the Brethren of the Sword was set up to fight for the Christian cause. Successful at first, the order became a major landowner in the region. But after a serious defeat by the Lithuanian army in 1237, it was absorbed into the Order of Teutonic Knights (see pages 32-33).

THE ALBIGENSIAN HERESY

FRANCE

0 — 100 miles
0 — 200 km

- Albi
Toulouse
Minerve
Muret
Béziers
Carcassonne
Peyrepertuse
Quéribus

Mediterranean Sea

SPAIN

Area of the Albigensian heresy

CRUSADES IN SPAIN

Muslims took over much of Spain in the early 8th century (see page 11). In 1212, Pope Innocent III launched a crusade against them. Preachers roused support in northern France, Italy, and Germany, and eventually a vast army, led by three Spanish kings, went to war. On July 17, 1212, they scored a crucial victory at Las Navas de Tolosa, north of the Guadalquivir River. This was the beginning of the end for the Muslims in Spain.

In his pro-crusade *Histoire Albigeoise*, Peter des Vaux describes how the people of Minerve, a village north of Carcassonne, were burned by Simon de Montfort (below) and his armies.

... Soon Simon of Montfort entered the castle and came to the house where the heretics were gathered together. Since he was a Catholic man and wished them all to be saved and come to recognize the truth, he first urged them to convert to the Catholic faith. But having no success, he had them dragged out of the castle. There were one hundred and forty or more **perfecti**. A huge fire was kindled and they were all thrown into it. It was not hard for our men to throw them in, because they were so obstinate in their wickedness that they all threw themselves in ...

The most strict and devoted Cathars.

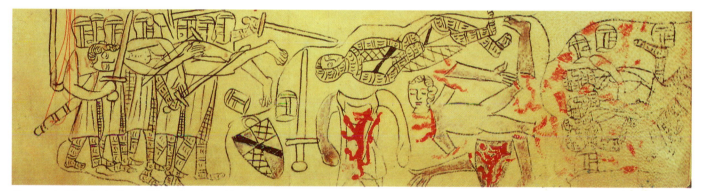

Simon de Montfort, the ruthless leader of the Crusade against the Cathars, was himself killed with extreme brutality.

The **"Children's Crusade" supposedly took place in 1212, when crowds of young people from France and Germany took ships for the east. This excerpt from Alberic of Trois Fontaine's *Chronicon* suggests a different story. Some historians think the crusade was a legend that grew out of the fact that in the 13th century many homeless families wandered around Europe.**

... In 1212 ... children from many different areas ... about thirty thousand of them, journeyed to Marseilles to take ship for Saracen lands. But vagrants and other wicked men who had joined them so damaged the whole venture that only a very few of such a great crowd came home: some perished at sea and others were sold as slaves. Of those who did manage to escape, some promised Pope Innocent III that they would cross the sea as crusaders when they came of age...

THE FIFTH AND SIXTH CRUSADES

In July 1216, Pope Innocent III died. The new pope, Honorius III, carried on Innocent's work of organizing another crusade to regain Jerusalem.

The Fifth Crusade arrived in Acre late in 1217. Its armies were undisciplined and no one gave them direction. Some crusaders went home. In 1218, more men arrived, and a plan was drawn up to attack Damietta on the River Nile in Egypt. The aim was to destroy the power of the Muslims there, weakening their ability to defend Jerusalem.

This 13th-century manuscript illustration shows the battle that took place at Damietta, Egypt, in 1218.

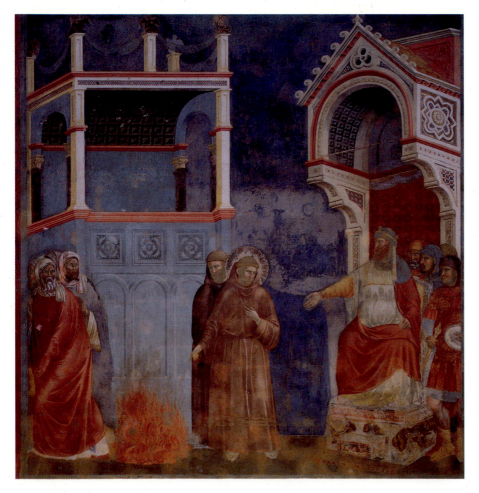

The crusaders sailed for Egypt in May 1218. When they arrived, they besieged a tower protecting the river channel leading to Damietta, took it, and continued to the city itself. Then they settled down for another siege.

Conditions inside and outside the city were grim—hunger and disease killed many. The Muslim ruler, al-Kamil, offered to compromise, even to give back the Kingdom of Jerusalem, but the crusade leader, Cardinal Pelagius, wanted total victory.

In 1219, the crusaders finally overran Damietta. However, victory turned into defeat when Pelagius led his armies down the Nile toward Cairo. In 1221, they

Saint Francis of Assisi went to Egypt in 1219, in the hope of arranging a truce between Crusaders and Muslims. Al-Kamil listened to him patiently, but then simply sent him away.

found themselves surrounded by Muslim troops and unable to retreat. Some of al-Kamil's troops attacked, others opened the gates that held back the flood waters of the river. The Fifth Crusade was drowned.

Christian failures in the Middle East did not deter one man from embarking on a sixth crusade. This man was the Western emperor, Frederick II. Frederick was brilliant and unconventional, a challenge to the authority of popes. He infuriated Pope Gregory IX so much by delaying his departure, leaving, then returning to Italy, that he was excommunicated. In spite of this, in 1229, Frederick succeeded where others had failed—he won back Jerusalem. This victory was not achieved by fighting, however, but by negotiation with Sultan al-Kamil.

The deal, designed to last for ten years, pleased no one. Militant Christians were angry because they wanted to fight and win, not come to peaceful agreements. The Muslims felt that al-Kamil had completely betrayed them. But future events would soon make the whole arrangement meaningless.

Emperor Frederick II.

 **This is how Ibn Al-Athir (see page 23) described the disastrous defeat of the crusaders on the banks of the River Nile:**

... The Franks were confident of their own strength and had brought with them provisions for only a few days, thinking that ... Egypt would fall into their hands, ... a detachment of Muslims crossed the river and opened the flood-gates. The river flooded most of the area and left the Franks with only one way out, along a narrow causeway. Al-Kamil threw a bridge over the Nile at Ashmun, and his troops crossed it and held the road along which the Franks would have to pass to reach Damietta. There was no escape. ...

THE LAST CRUSADES

In the early 13th century, the Mongols of Central Asia, led by Genghis Khan, began their rise to power. As they stormed west, they drove other peoples ahead of them. Among these were the Khorezmian Turks, who in 1244 captured Jerusalem.

In Europe, the saintly king of France, Louis IX, was planning another, seventh, crusade. He intended to gain Jerusalem by seizing Egypt first. Louis and an army of about 3,000 knights reached Damietta in 1249. They quickly took the city and pressed on in triumph. In 1250 they met the Muslims in battle at Mansourah. Victory turned to defeat, then disaster as Louis was taken prisoner by the Mameluks, the fierce fighting men who formed the backbone of the Egyptian armies.

Louis was set free later in 1250 after payment of a ransom and the return of Damietta to the Muslims. He then made his way to the Holy

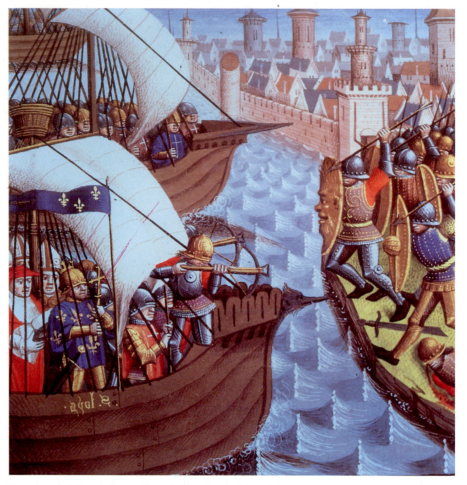

The siege of Damietta by French king Louis IX and his troops in 1249.

Trainee Mameluks practice their sword skills.

Land, where he stayed for four years. During that time, he tried to persuade the Mongols to help him in his struggle against the Muslims. However, the Mongols acted alone. Beginning in 1256, they conquered city after city.

In 1260, the Mongols and the Mameluks, who had seized power in Egypt, clashed. At the Battle of Ayn Jalut, the Asian armies were stopped dead in their tracks. In 1261, they suffered a second defeat at Homs. Now it was the Mameluks, led by their sultan,

Baybars, who demolished the Holy Land. Louis attempted to hold back the flood, but he died on the Eighth Crusade, in Tunisia.

The Mameluks gradually eroded the Christians' territory until they were left clinging to the coast from Tyre down to Jaffa. Finally a new Mameluk sultan, Qala'un, expelled them even from there. Tripoli fell in 1289. Qala'un died in 1291, and his son, Al-Ashraf Kamil, took Acre. Sidon and Beirut also fell in 1291. It was all over. The Holy Land was lost.

THE KNIGHTS HOSPITALLER

The order of the Knights Templar did not continue for long after the loss of the Holy Land (see pages 32-33), but the Hospitallers built a new role for themselves elsewhere. First they moved to Cyprus, where they already owned land. Then, between 1306 and 1309, they won the island of Rhodes from the Greeks (right). From this base, they fought sea battles against Muslims from Egypt and Turkey. They also set up a hospital and pilgrim hostels there. In 1522, Turks drove the Hospitallers out of Rhodes, and in 1530 they moved to Malta, where they remained until the French emperor, Napoleon, forced them to leave in 1798.

 The French nobleman Jean de Joinville accompanied Louis IX on the Seventh Crusade. He greatly admired the king, and knew him as a friend as well as a ruler. In Jean's book, *The Life of Saint Louis* (Louis was made a saint after his death), he explains how King Louis made arrangements for his release from capture in Egypt.

Coins first made in Byzantium.

... When the Saracens had seen that they could not prevail over our good king with threats, they had come back to him and asked him how much money he was prepared to pay the sultan, and whether he would also surrender Damietta. The king had replied that if the sultan was willing to accept a reasonable sum he would send and advise the queen to pay that amount for their ransom. "How is it," they had asked, "that you won't tell us definitely whether you'll do this?" The king had answered that he did not know whether or not the queen would consent, since, as his consort, she was mistress of her actions. So the councilors had gone to confer with the sultan, and had later returned to tell the king that if the queen was prepared to pay a million gold **bezants**—a sum amounting to five hundred thousand livres in our currency—their master would set him at liberty....

CONCLUSION

More crusades followed the loss of the Holy Land, but all were unsuccessful. When a new Muslim power, the Ottoman Turks, surged west in the 15th century, still more crusades tried to stop them. In 1453, the Turks seized Constantinople and destroyed the Byzantine Empire. The crusade that Pope Pius II called in response failed for lack of support, and the crusading ideal went into decline.

During the Middle Ages, Christian scholars struggled to justify the violence of the crusades, relying on the "just war" idea set out by St. Augustine in the 5th century. Augustine said that Christians should wage war only if three conditions were met. First, the cause of the war had to be just, for example, if Christian lands were threatened. Second, the cause had to be proclaimed by someone with authority to do so. Third, the war had to be fought with "right intention," not out of greed or revenge.

The scholars argued that Muslim occupation of the Holy Land was a just cause, that the Pope had the right to proclaim war, and that the expulsion of the Muslims was a right intention. Many believed that crusades were not only just but holy, fought on behalf of Christ. Others questioned whether Christians ever had the right to kill.

For Muslims, there was less contradiction between belief and action. Islam permitted the use of violence (see pages 10-11) and

The Siege of Constantinople, 1453.

Muhammad himself had been a warrior. Some Islamic scholars taught that while Muslims lived in the House of Submission (*Dar el-Islam*), non-Muslims lived in the House of War (*Dar el-Harb*) and could be attacked for the good of Islam.

During the crusades, thousands of ordinary people fought for their faith, sacrificing homes, land, and lives. However, on both sides, pure motives were often mixed with intolerance and greed, and there was appalling savagery. The crusades achieved little. By the late 13th century, the Christians had lost the Holy Land. By the mid-15th century, they had lost Byzantium, too, and the Turks were still heading west.

Nurses walk past the St. John Ophthalmic Hospital in Jerusalem.

THE LEGACY OF THE CRUSADES
The meeting of East and West during the crusades had lasting effects, including the religiously motivated violence that still scars the Middle East. But some important ideals of the crusader era still exist. The documents below highlight two of them.

The British Order of St. John, descended from the Knights Hospitaller, today teaches and provides first aid. It also runs the St. John Ophthalmic (Eye) Hospital in Jerusalem.
Excerpts from the statutes of the Hospital of St. John, 1177 to 1187 (1), and the 1888 royal charter (2) show that the order's humanitarian aims have changed little over the centuries.

1 ... the ... Holy House of the Hospital has been accustomed to receive in kindness sick men and women, and to have doctors who are in charge of the sick, and are accustomed to make the necessary syrups for the said sick...

2 ... [The aims of the Order are] works of humanity and charity in the relief of sickness, distress, suffering, and danger without distinction of nationality or creed, and the extension of the great principle of the Order, *Pro Utilitate Hominum*. ...

"For the Service of Mankind." The other motto of the Order is Pro Fide, "For the Faith."

The United Nations was established in 1945. Its charter attempted to define the idea of the "just war" for the modern world. These excerpts are from the UN Charter:

This means invading some or all of another state's land.

Article 1
The Purposes of the United Nations are:
1. To maintain international peace and security, and to that end: to take effective collective measures for the prevention and removal of threats to the peace, and for the suppression of acts of aggression or other breaches of the peace ...

Article 2
4. All Members shall refrain in their international relations from the **threat or use of force against the territorial integrity** or political independence of any state, or in any other manner inconsistent with the Purposes of the United Nations. ...

GLOSSARY

Armenian a member of a Christian church founded in Armenia in the 3rd century A.D. Its leader was called an *exarch* and its beliefs were similar to those of the Greek Orthodox Church (see below). This church still exists.

battering ram a huge wooden beam, often covered with iron at one end. Besieging armies used these to smash a way through walls and gates of cities.

Bosphorus the 17-mi (27-km)-long channel of water that separates the European and Asian parts of Turkey. Constantinople stood on its western, European, shore.

caliph a title first used by the direct successors of the Prophet Muhammad, but later adopted by Muslim rulers in Egypt, Turkey, and elsewhere. It comes from the Arabic word *khalifa*, "successor."

caravan a group of travelers with their animals and goods. Arab merchants with cargoes on camels often crossed Middle Eastern deserts during the time of the crusades.

Cardinal a high-ranking priest of the Roman Catholic Church.

chain mail armor made of linked iron rings. Knights often wore a mail coat (hauberk), leggings, gloves with leather palms, and a neck guard.

chronicler a person who keeps a record (chronicle) of events.

citadel a thick-walled fortress where armies defended themselves and their cities from attack.

crossbow a type of bow held horizontally. Crossbows fire bolts instead of arrows.

deposed removed from power.

doctrine a set of beliefs approved by a religious authority.

dynasty a family that rules a country or region for many generations.

emirate a territory governed by an Islamic ruler called an emir. Emir comes from the Arabic *amir*, "commander."

excommunicated expelled from the Roman Catholic Church.

feudal government a type of medieval government in which each level of society granted land to the one below it in return for military and other service. Kings granted land to lords, lords to knights, knights to peasants etc., so that they were all linked.

fresco a wall picture created by painting on damp plaster.

Goths a people that originally came from Scandinavia, then settled near the Black Sea in about the 2nd century A.D. There were two main groups, the eastern Ostrogoths and the western Visigoths. They raided southern Europe from the 4th century A.D. In 410, the Visigoths sacked Rome.

Greek Orthodox Church the name given to all the eastern churches that officially broke away from the western, Roman Catholic, Church (see below) in A.D. 1054. Also known as the Eastern Orthodox Church or the Orthodox Church.

heretical holding beliefs that do not agree with the official teaching of the Roman Catholic Church or other religious organizations.

Holy Land the part of the ancient Middle East known as Palestine, where many events related in the Bible took place, including the life and death of Jesus Christ. The area is now divided between Israel and Jordan.

Holy Roman Empire see Western Empire, below.

infidel a critical term used by members of a particular religion to describe a person who rejects their beliefs. The word means "unfaithful."

inquisition an organization that sought out and punished people who held beliefs that the Roman Catholic Church considered heretical.

Jacobite a member of a Syrian church that was founded in A.D. 451.

jihad an Arabic word that means "struggling" and "fighting." It refers to physical struggle, such as defending Islam from its enemies, and mental struggle as people try to conquer their own sins.

lance a weapon consisting of a long, thin pole with a pointed head.

mangonel a huge catapult used to hurl missiles.

Maronite a member of a Syrian church founded in about the 7th century A.D. Maro, after whom the church is named, was a 5th-century Syrian monk.

mercenary a soldier hired by a foreign army who fights for money rather than for his country or a just cause.

Mesopotamia an area of south-west Asia between the Tigris River and the Euphrates River. It now forms part of Iraq.

Middle Ages the time between the fall of the Roman Empire in the 5th century A.D. and the fall of Constantinople in 1453, that is, between the end of the ancient and the beginning of the modern world.

minaret a mosque tower with one or more balconies. Muslims are called to prayer from minarets five times every day.

Mongol a member of a Central Asian people whose tribes were united by Genghis Khan in A.D. 1206. The Mongols were driven from the Holy Land in the mid-13th century. Their vast empire, which covered much of Russia and China, collapsed in the early 15th century.

mystical a religious experience of God that is said to come directly through prayer and other spiritual activities.

naphtha a form of crude oil (petroleum).

pagan a person who follows a religion other than Judaism, Christianity, or Islam.

Patriarch the title of the most important bishops in the Greek Orthodox Church. The most senior bishop of the Byzantine Church was the Patriarch of Constantinople.

Qur'an The Muslim holy book, containing the revelations received from the Archangel Gabriel by the Prophet Muhammad. The Qur'an is divided into 114 *suras* ("chapters").

Roman Catholic Church the Christian church whose leader is the Pope and whose headquarters are in Rome. It split from the Greek Orthodox Church (see above) in A.D. 1054.

scaling ladder a tall ladder used to climb (scale) high walls.

Shi'ite Muslim a member of the Shiah branch of Islam. Shi'ites believe that Ali, the Prophet Muhammad's son-in-law, was his rightful successor.

statute a rule about how an organization should be run.

Sunni Muslim a member of the Sunni branch of Islam. Sunnis believe that Abu Bakr, the Prophet Muhammad's father-in-law, was his rightful successor. They follow a set of Islamic laws, the *Sunna* (rule), which they believe developed from Muhammad's own teachings and actions.

United Nations an international organization formed in 1945 after World War II. Its main aims are to promote peace, security, and cooperation among the countries of the world. The headquarters of the United Nations are in New York City.

Vikings warriors and traders from Denmark, Sweden, and Norway who traveled by sea to countries such as Britain, France, and Russia from the 8th to the 11th centuries A.D. They raided many of the places that they reached, but they also set up some peaceful settlements, for example, in York.

vizier a title given to important Muslim officials such as the chief minister of a sultan or other ruler.

Western Empire a European empire that lasted from about A.D. 800 to 1806. It was called the Western Empire to distinguish it from the Eastern, Byzantine, Empire. In the 13th century, it became known as the Holy Roman Empire, now sometimes used to describe the empire at all stages of its history.

INDEX